NOT INVENTED HERE

cross-industry innovation

T0304984

RAMON VULLINGS & MARC HELEVEN

Copyright © 2015
Ramon Vullings & Marc Heleven

www.crossindustryinnovation.com

NOT INVENTED HERE
cross–industry innovation
ISBN 978-90-6369-379-4
5th printing 2020

Find the e-book on Amazon and in the iBooks Store!

Copy Editor: Sarina Ruiter–Bouwhuis
Graphic Design: We Make Graphics
www.wemakegraphics.be

BIS Publishers
Building Het Sieraad
Postjesweg 1
1057 DT Amsterdam
The Netherlands
T +31 (0)20 515 02 30
bis@bispublishers.com
www.bispublishers.com

"If you look only within your industry for best practices, you'll find only what your competitors are already doing. To do better than competitors, you have to look beyond. In Not Invented Here Ramon and Marc masterfully unpack the process of borrowing and adapting ideas from outside your industry. A must-read for innovation-seeking managers." Niraj Dawar — Author of 'TILT: Shifting Your Strategy from Products to Customers', Professor of Marketing at Ivey Business School, Canada

"Taking business lessons from other sectors' cross-industry innovation is something which is close to my heart. I've done research on what businesses can learn from the creative industries, and recommend Not Invented Here as a cool visual guide to help you cross your own borders. " Jamie Anderson — Professor of Innovation Management at Antwerp Management School & Founding Partner, Connected Visions.

"Go beyond multidisciplinary to interdisciplinary."
Tom Kelley — Author of 'The Ten Faces of Innovation' and General Manager of IDEO

"By using practical examples, Ramon & Marc provide an excellent read on this highly interesting topic. Being active in different sectors myself, I can fully acknowledge the importance of cross-industry innovation, as I constantly encourage my employees to get inspiration from other industries." Peter Kuppens — CEO of Maxxelli Group China

"The only book on stealing which is legal! Copy, Adapt and Paste your way into new innovations for your industry." Martin de Ruiter — Manager Account Management, FloraHolland

"Cross-industry innovation is critical, as other industries' successes in impossible missions & challenges makes our industry rethink the innovation matrix and open new horizons." Mel de Vogue — CFO & co-CEO of Tessenderlo Group

"A really great & innovative book to inspire cross-industry innovation. Helps to think outside the box with many illustrations." Dr. Bernold Beckenbauer — Global Innovation Manager, Linde Healthcare

"Not invented here is spot on! It illustrates exactly what today's companies and leaders need to do: to look outside and learn from others. This book provides great examples and practical tips to get started." Stan Steverink — Director Leadership Development, CircleRadius

Contents

= TOOL

Looking for positive alternatives

A book like this does not emerge from a library; it has resulted from hundreds of conversations, innovation projects and experiments with clients over many years, across many industries.

Creativity is just connecting things

We — the authors — believe there are positive alternatives to many of the challenges we face. More elegant solutions already exist somewhere else — in another area, another industry, another sector — yet they are not recognised as a possibility. Hence the title of this book:

Not Invented Here

Referring to the phenomenon of people blocking out ideas from the *outside*, it also indicates that there are beautiful alternatives everywhere just waiting to be introduced to your context.

This book aims to be a joyful guide, using inspiring stories, challenging thoughts and many practical tools. From cover to cover or at random: no matter how you dive in, insights are bound to arise.

We would like to invite you to this quest called *cross-industry innovation*, learning from other sectors, not just to think outside the box — but even more importantly — to think outside of your industry. We hope to inspire and enable you by developing your *match sensitivity* to make even better connections.

Enjoy the journey!

Ramon & Marc

cross-industry innovation

Lessons from other sectors

What can a hospital learn from a hotel?
What can a car manufacturer learn from
the video game industry?
What can a chemical company learn
from a festival organiser?

Organisations need more radical and game-changing innovation to be able to meet the challenges they will be facing.

Today, innovation is seen as one of the main driving forces for growth, development and profitability. The problem is that — in many cases — innovation is an extrapolation of the current situation. Incremental improvement is necessary and beneficial, yet it is not enough to gain a real competitive advantage or to find game-changing ways of working.

As most industries are quite mature, it is hard to generate major innovations as most products, services and business models have largely been shaped by the mindset of their respective industries. Best practice thinking in management has optimised *(economic)* sector operations, so radical innovation

— we call them *next practices* — will most likely come from other sectors.

"Cross-industry innovation is a clever way to jump-start your innovation efforts by drawing analogies and transferring approaches between contexts, beyond the borders of your own industry, sector, area or domain."

These analogies can be drawn at various levels, from products to services, to processes, to strategies, to business models, to culture and leadership. The key is to develop your ability to make more effective connections — i.e. your *match sensitivity* — and see the opportunities available.

_____

Cross-industry innovation is like a springboard for innovation. So go ahead — dive in!

Cross-industry innovation in action

Let's take a look at some examples, starting with material products (automotive, sports and utilities products), followed by an example related to a service (alternative use for phone booths) and finally an example concerning an experience (MRI scanner in a hospital).

BMW's iDrive system

BMW's iDrive system was inspired by the video game industry. The iDrive system is a solution to operate the relatively complex navigation in a simple way — while being able to keep your eyes on the road.

Nike Shox

Nike Shox shoes were adapted from Formula One racing shock absorbers. The unique feature of this approach is that — in addition to shock absorption — they actually spring back. Hence providing extra power, according to Nike.

WORX TWIST & GO

The WORX QBIT Twist & Go automatic screwdriver was inspired by the design of a revolver. Never lose your screw bits again. It actually gives the device a pretty sleek appearance.

Red London phone boxes on Tottenham Court Road are converted into free solar-powered mobile phone charging points.

Don't be afraid of an MRI scan

A magnetic resonance imaging *(MRI)* scanner is quite an impressive machine. It makes annoying bonking sounds and you are expected to lie completely still inside it. A stressful experience for adults, let alone for children.

To make matters even worse for children — parents are not allowed in the room when the machine is active. Many kids get scared and start to cry and move around — resulting in a high percentage of incorrect images. In many cases, the doctors resort to anaesthesia.

Doug Dietz — principal designer for high-tech medical imaging systems at **GE Healthcare** — attended a Stanford training on design thinking *(powered by IDEO)*, which would finally help him in his quest to make MRIs less frightening for young children. He finally discovered that the real problem was the experience.

The *GE Adventure Series* was born. A themed experience — starting of with storytelling by means of a video and consistently upheld throughout the process — down to a complete overhaul in appearance of the MRI and CT machines and the actual room. The adventure series even has multiple themes to choose from, such as pirates, space, jungle, coral reef and safari.

By really stepping into the shoes of a child and combining this perspective with inspiration from a completely different sector *(in this case the entertainment industry)* — they were able to turn a scary experience for children into a true adventure, and at the same time ensure a significant increase in the number of correct scans upon the first try.

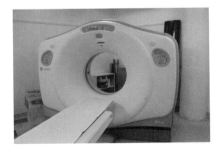

How might you be able to transform your product or service experience into a true adventure?

Going from best to next practices

Best practices are great; you need them as a basis for running your organisation and optimising your operations. However, if you wish to achieve a true competitive edge, it's simply not enough anymore.

Best practice thinking is largely limited to the prevailing mind set and market for your product. In other words: best practices are limited to the current scope of your industry or processes.

Relevancy of ideas

best practices

next practices

Time

Next practices are about new markets, new concepts, new ways of working, new products and services, smart extensions, imagination, courage and entrepreneurship.

Next practices break patterns. They radically alter your processes and change the game by disrupting your industry. Think of **Ryanair** doing away with paper tickets and allocated seating or **Cirque du Soleil** creating a circus without animals.

Now, how does one go from best to next?

By allowing yourself to step into the unknown and explore places and areas you've never really investigated before. Conduct smart research, observe, make new connections and experiment with different combinations. That is what cross-industry innovation is all about.

Go through the craziness phase

Initially, your environment and colleagues might think you've gone mad.

"What on earth can one learn from a totally different sector or even nature? You can't be serious."

At times, you may even think you are going nuts yourself. This is perfectly fine. In fact, it is quite a necessary phase in the whole process.

You need to go through the craziness to be able to jump out of the limiting box of *best practices* to enter the world of *next practices*. A world of opportunity lies ahead: so many things still waiting to be discovered — so many insights yet to be stumbled upon — just because they have other names and descriptions in other areas.

Now, where will you go next?

Cross-industry best to next practices

INDUSTRY WITH INNOVATION QUESTION	ISSUE	BEST PRACTICES
Events & conferences	People arrive late	Start times at 9.00 start – 10.15 coffee – 12.30 lunch
Utilities	Lowering maintenance costs for power plants	Classic process improvement
Healthcare	Problematic baby birth in rural areas and less developed countries	Natural delivery *(yet no backup in case of complications)*
Building demolition	Mid-city demolition is complex due to debris and fallout	Use of explosives and fallout
Bioengineering / Chemistry	Accurate test setups are expensive	Lab setups and Petri dishes

DESIRED EFFECT	INSPIRATION FROM ANOTHER INDUSTRY	NEXT PRACTICE
People arrive on time *(sense of urgency)*	Railway timetable	Start times at 9.03 start – 10.17 coffee – 12.34 lunch
Balance risk & costs	Ryanair, EasyJet, Thomas Cook	Use airplane safety check procedures approach
Safe delivery of babies	Cork-out-of-the-bottle party trick	The Odon device *(plastic bag with suction)* to help deliver babies safely during complications
A cleaner method for building demolition in cities	Japanese game where blocks are hit away from the bottom	Tear down buildings by removing the ground floor and then lowering the building
Easy and programmable setups without the use of a full lab	A toy music box with winding mechanism	A €5 chemistry box with programmable and accurate delivery

Concept
Combine
Create

Cross-industry innovation is a clever way to jump-start your innovation efforts by drawing analogies and transferring approaches between contexts, beyond the borders of your own industry, sector, area or domain.

So how do you actually achieve cross-industry innovation?

1. Concept

2. Combine

3. Create

In order to make effective use of a practice from another sector or area in the right way, one should master three things: conceptualisation skills, the ability to combine and, ultimately, to make the pieces fit.

Remember that cross-industry analogies can be drawn at various levels — from products to services, to processes, to strategies, to business models, to culture and leadership.

**The model:
CONCEPT – COMBINE – CREATE**

1. CONCEPT
The ability to conceptualise. Become more flexible in asking questions on multiple levels. Play with abstraction levels. Get help from curators and conduct in-depth research. — **Ask: why?**

2. COMBINE
The ability to make smart combinations. Use lateral thinking to find *matches* and similarities. Seeing the *(potential)* parallels in order to organise a profitable meeting of contexts. Search for elegant inspiration. — **Ask: what if?**

3. CREATE
The ability to make it fit your situation. It is not survival of the fittest, but rather the best fitting. This step ensures that you make it fit: adapt, modify, customise it to your situation. Adopt what you can, adapt the rest. — **Ask: how?**

**The magic:
Develop your match sensitivity**

In the next chapters we will focus on developing these skills, provide you with smart cross-industry strategies and — in the process — increase your match sensitivity, to enable you to make better connections.

What's holding us back?

We live inside our sector silos. **We don't recognise that industry borders are blurring.** We are blind to or underestimate the power of small disruptive companies. **As a _Top 3 player_ we feel very comfortable.** We overestimate our position in our sector. **The unknown of _what's out there_ leads to insecurity and makes us choose for the familiar.** We regard ideas and concepts as _what is_ not as _what could be_. **As a public company our focus is on short-term success, so we use proven methods to reach our targets.** We perceive the world through the lens of our industry. **We extrapolate using the past as a reference for the future.** We are totally up-to-date on what is happening in _our_ industry. **We want to be the _original_ creators of _our_ innovations.**

not invented here !

Not invented here?
Already done there!

The potential of ideas and approaches from other areas is tremendous. Still only very few organisations apply cross-industry innovation strategies in any kind of structured way.

Why do we hold back?

Why don't we look beyond our borders more often? We seem to search for solutions in the areas we already know.

Not invented here

The *not invented here* syndrome actually holds people back from using ideas, concepts and approaches from other domains.

It's our plea to embrace other people's and other sector's ideas and build upon them. This way *not invented here* becomes *already invented there.*

Now let's use these insights as building blocks for our challenges!

Cross-industry innovation readiness check

Use the not invented here bingo card to check your organisation's level of: *not invented here*.

The higher the score, the more work needed!
Hand out a few copies of this book.

Download this poster and more – for free – at
crossindustryinnovation.com/tools.

NOT INVENTED HERE – BINGO

Yes, but…	Has been tried before	Our customers won't accept it	We are too small for that	We are not Apple
We left that business years ago	We can invent it ourselves	We are the market leader	That's only a start-up	It already exists
Let's develop it ourselves	The new guy doesn't know the rules yet		We have our own R&D department	This won't survive in our sector
It's against the rules	Impossible to make money with that	We are not in that business	It is not designed for that	That's too simple
The boss won't like it	The market is not ready for this	Since when did you become an expert at…	Not for our department	Open innovation is a hype

WHAT'S YOUR STRATEGY?

DON'T
COPY – PASTE

COPY — ADAPT — PASTE

COPY **ADAPT** PASTE

Enrich
Customise
Take 1 element
Experiment
Re-imagine
Double
Modify
Blend
Learn
Break
Move
Fuse
Play
...

CHAPTER

2

the art of
questioning

A great idea is not an invention, it's a discovery.

Cross-industry innovation is the commitment we make to the process of asking questions, **combining elements, finding patterns and testing concepts.**

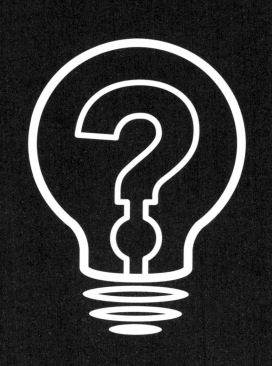

The power of questions

Cross-industry innovation starts with asking more and better questions. Questions allow you to conceptualise a situation, which is the first step in concept-combine-create.

In his book: *A More Beautiful Question*, **Warren Berger** describes the crucial role questions play for innovation.

For cross-industry innovation we wish to create organisations which have a *culture of inquiry.* Therefore, we need people to ask more powerful questions.

We can take a cue from **Eric Vogts'** book: *The Art of Powerful Questions.*

Powerful questions:
* generate curiosity in the listener
* are thought-provoking
* surface underlying assumptions
* channel attention
* focus inquiry
* stimulate reflective conversation
* generate energy
* evoke more questions

"If I had an hour to solve a problem and my life depended on the solution, I would spend the first 55 minutes determining the proper question to ask, for once I know the proper question, I could solve the problem in less than five minutes."

— *Albert Einstein*

On the next pages we outline some beautiful questions that aim to spark your cross-industry insights.

Beautiful questions

Swapping players is common in the sports industry. Why don't companies do this with employees?

Why can't smart energy meters / thermostats select the right energy supplier for that moment?

Why don't cities work more like forests?

What if there were no physical stores, cinemas and banks?

Why don't rules have expiry dates?

Why do they give you a Jaguar for a test drive but you can't sleep in a house you want to buy!

Why do we get previews and samples everywhere yet do we still order from text-based menus in restaurants?

Why does a patient get lost in a hospital, while in retail the customer's routing is a true science?

Why is it so much harder to vote for a politician, than for the next top model?

Why can I get a full outline of my bank transactions and not from my supermarket?

Why can I buy advertising space per centimetre yet I can't buy variable leg room in an airplane?

More
beautiful
questions

Inquiry enables us to
organise our thinking
around what we
don't know.

Why do you have to wait for hospital operation planning, while you can arrange a flight to Australia for tomorrow yourself?

Why can't people choose what *(part of)* their tax money is spent on?

Why are traffic jams so hard to solve, while international container shipping is a nearly flawless process?

Why are cars left unused for nearly 20 hours a day?

What if robots were your co-workers?

What if your mobile phone told you when you've eaten enough, rather than your stomach?

Why is there so much fuss about digital patient data security, while secure online banking is already so commonplace?

Why is there a business model dedicated to the waiting experience in airports, while it can be so unpleasant in hospitals?

Why do we try to beat or copy nature with systems and techniques, instead of joining nature in its proven concept?

Why does a plumber respond to your needs with an open intake and do restaurants still make you choose from a menu?

____

Find at least 3 *beautiful questions* for your industry

Ask (better) questions

DO	DON'T
CURIOSITY	INDIFFERENCE
REFLECTION	REACTION
REVEAL ASSUMPTIONS	EXTEND BIASES
CREATIVITY	AGREEMENT
ENERGY	STALL
ENGAGEMENT	DISTRACTION
TRUST	SUSPICION
MEANINGFUL	TRIVIAL
TRIGGER MORE QUESTIONS	DEAD ENDS

Jargon? Ask questions in the first 100 days

Industry borders are pretty well defined by the use of jargon — the language that people in a specific sector commonly use and understand. The trick is to make sure you interview new people — ask them about their observations, what they think is strange or special — before their first 100 days are over, after that people tend to be in full compliance *(read: understand the jargon)*.

"In Germany — companies such as Daimler, Bayer, Siemens and SAP all have an entire department of Grundsatzfragen (in English: a department of Fundamental Questions). It's clear these companies see questioning as a strategic asset."

Tips for better questions

- Refuse to accept the current reality
- Invite outsiders to ask questions about your work and your industry
- Imagine the perfect situation
- Detect real customer insights by analysing their actual behaviour
- Challenge everything; don't base yourself on industry assumptions
- Most complaints can be translated into positive questions
- Time-travel and ask yourself questions about your business now
- As children are the R&D department of humanity: perceive with naive *(child-like)* eyes

The best way
to develop ideas
is to look at
other places.

Spend time learning from other markets, other sectors. Apply the best ideas from one sector into another.

— *Frabrizio Freda*, CEO of The Estée Lauder Companies Inc.

Ask other companies

Consider how other companies would tackle your situation.

How would IKEA organise subway routing?
Would there be clear arrows on the floor?

How would Disney design a waiting room?
Would there be someone telling stories?

How would Virgin sell elderly care?
Would you get elderly wildly enthusiastic about their care?

How would Google organise your administration?
Would everything end up in one basket automatically scanned and presented to you on the best date to approve payments?

How would Airbnb provide road assistance?
Would you be able to see in which houses around you people have skills and tools available and at which costs they provide them?

How would Zara organise harvesting?

How would medication be sold via iTunes?

How would LinkedIn organise civil registration?

How would Karl Lagerfeld design police uniforms?

How would Bayern München arrange money transfers?

How would Amazon design the political voting process?

How would MTV organise the labour market?

How would NASA lower your energy bill?

How would Kickstarter divide subsidies?

How would NIKE arrange education?

———

How would you do it?

TOOL

The art of looking sideways

All cross-industry innovation efforts start with a question.

Asking the right question is an art, and to practice any art you need good tools. This tool for looking sideways helps you to find the right variation of your key question.

Let's look at an example of **Albert Heijn**, a large super market chain in The Netherlands. One of the questions they asked themselves was: "*How might we reduce the waiting time at the checkout counters?*" A good question, one would think. At the same time, sticking to this question severely limits the range of possible solutions. So how might we break it open?

The diagram on the next page shows you how to structure a problem. Asking "*What is the purpose?*" brings you to a higher conceptual level. Asking "*In what ways?*" brings you down to a more concrete level. Moving sideways in the diagram helps you to redefine the question in other manners and opens up a whole world of possibilities and links with other industries that have already addressed similar questions before.

Now, it's time for the art of looking sideways!

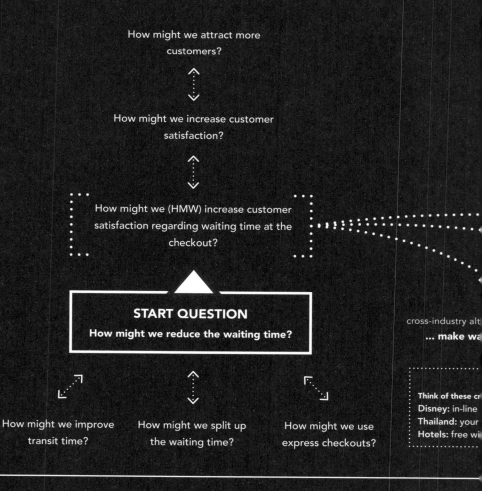

CLASSICAL PROBLEM SOLVING

How might we attract more customers?

How might we increase customer satisfaction?

How might we (HMW) increase customer satisfaction regarding waiting time at the checkout?

START QUESTION
How might we reduce the waiting time?

How might we improve transit time?

How might we split up the waiting time?

How might we use express checkouts?

cross-industry alt
... make wa

Think of these cro
Disney: in-line
Thailand: your
Hotels: free wi

CROSS-INDUSTR

The art of looking sideways

1. Define your start question
2. Transcend the question and ask *"Why?"* or *"What is the purpose?"* — bringing you to a higher level of conceptualisation.
3. From this helicopter view you will be able to move sideways in the diagram, which will help you to redefine the question in a cross-industry way. This opens up a whole world of possibilities and links with other industries that have already addressed similar questions before.
4. Think of the various industries that have implemented your solution already.

2

– **How might we:** re pleasant?

cross-industry alternative 2 – **How might we:** ... make waiting useful?

3

cross-industry alternative 3 – **How might we:** ... eliminate waiting time?

2

y solutions
ent
wait for you

2

Think of these cross-industry solutions
Educational: in-line infotainment
Networking: queues based on interests
Health: fitness waiting *(to burn calories)*

3

Think of these cross-industry solutions
Airport: self-scanning and checkout
Internet: home delivery
Catering: butler service

someone else has solved your problem

No one lives long enough to learn everything by starting from scratch.

— Brian Tracy

Someone else has solved your problem

————————

Why didn't I think of that (before)?
— is something people say when they encounter an obvious solution to a problem or when they meet an entrepreneur who came up with a brilliant new value proposition.

The same goes for your own topics; someone else has most likely been working on a challenge similar to the one you are facing.

Look out!
The *not invented here* syndrome actually blinds you from seeing the obvious, which is that other people have already addressed your situation — be it in another context.

The key is to find this other person. This chapter focuses on how to expand and use your knowledge network and on finding your curators — people who are already doing a lot of groundwork for you.

Spot the changes and (re)search
As industries are transforming *(blurring, fading and expanding)* we see totally new roles appear. In this chapter we provide you with tips for spotting the trends and finally we will also provide you with hands-on tools for greatly improving your internet (re)search.

————

The secret might well be hidden in another sector!

IF THIS IS YOUR CHALLENGE ...

Faster machine maintenance in a factory?

A better experience in a hotel or hospital?

Declining sales of physical newspapers?

Smaller yet more multi-functional teams?

Better work planning?

More efficient use of office or storage space?

Optimise maintenance costs versus risk management?

Wow your next customer day?

An insurance brokers membership?

... DISCOVER INSIGHTS IN THESE AREAS

Formula 1 pit stop

Amusement parks

Online music & mobile apps

Submarine crew

International container shipping

International Space Station *(ISS)*

Low-cost airlines

Tomorrowland festival

Motorcycle club: Harley Owners Group

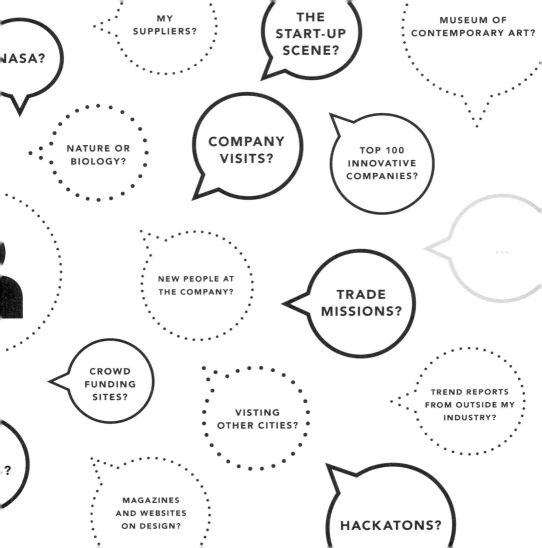

Your galaxy of knowledge

1. Your knowledge

2. Your team's knowledge

3. Your company's knowledge

4. Competitive industries knowledge

5. Non-competitive industries knowledge

6. All knowledge

7. The unknown

Find your curators

Look at the world of knowledge and networks available to you. It's great to have access to literally a world of information — yet all this information can be overwhelming. It's your network and the curators in your network who will actually guide you through.

Don't look for factual information — but look for the ultimate expert *(person, organisation, university, etc.)* instead. The beautiful work curators do, is converting data into accessible knowledge.

Take your time to look for your curators — as they will vary per question and are sometimes very well hidden *(in another sector)*. In addition — they might use completely different jargon.

Good curators are COOL

The best curators are COOL: Curating Out Of Love. These people craft their knowledge and insight by means of websites, blogs and books like a sculptor creates a sculpture.

So, who's a good curator?

- Someone who has been gathering, carefully selecting and organising information on a specific domain.

- Someone who is passionately been cracking the same problems you are tackling right now.

- Someone who creates concepts based on patterns and principles they discovered themselves.

"Netflix is really watching… you! Before buying shows, Netflix checks piracy websites to make sure people are interested."

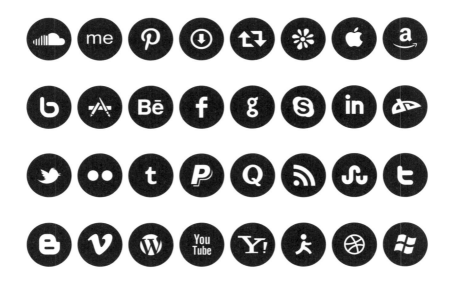

Use your knowledge network

Social media tools like LinkedIn, Facebook, Twitter, Open Innovation platforms and idea contests can do amazing things by offering you the chance to do research or to pose your question to the community.

You will be amazed at how many people *(many you don't even know)* are willing to help. In addition, the quality of the information provided will often truly surprise you.

These insights help you to start combining and creating your cross-industry innovations.

Reach out!

Use your network to find insights and clues, actually use your networks' network to find them.

Ask a question on Twitter and use the hashtag **#daretoask** — which refers to *Dare to Ask* — the English translation of the Dutch initiative *Durf te Vragen (#dtv)*. This hashtag was invented to encourage people to ask any question they might have and invite answers from the entire Twitter base.

Join LinkedIn groups from other industries that inspire you — post a question and see the magic of that network unfold.

Don't forget **slideshare.net** *(YouTube for PowerPoint presentations)* for great slide shows on just about any subject. SlideShare is the home base for many fantastic curators. Take for example **Peter Fisk** who creates true cross-border SlideShares on brands and marketing from all over the world.

Also look for experts in your own organisation. You might be amazed at how many departments can still learn from other departments in your organisation. The only problem is, people usually don't ask enough questions.

We can only connect the dots that we collect.

— *Amanda Palmer*

WAKE–UP CALL

Fading futures

The artist Christopher Locke created modern fossils to illustrate the rapid ageing of technology.

Wake up if you operate in one of these businesses

Petrol-engined vehicles – Wallets – National currencies – Libraries – DVDs – Secretaries – Bookshops – Middleman – Insurance brokers – Postal services – Gas stations – Toll road industry …

What is your industry's time of extinction?

10 disappearing jobs that won't exist in 10 years' time

Retail cashier – Telemarketer – Freight storage provider – Newspaper deliverer – Travel agent – Postal worker – Taxi dispatcher – Typist – Librarian – Social media manager – Meter reader …

Which jobs will disappear in your industry?

The dinosaur list

50 dead products and how to stay off this list
Gijs van Wulfen — a key LinkedIn influencer — made an inspiring list of 50 dinosaur products and services on the verge of going extinct soon or which have completely disappeared already.

Check whether your product is set to end up on the dinosaur list.

1. Amateur radio
2. Answering machines
3. Bank affiliates
4. Bar soap
5. Board games
6. Bookstores
7. Boombox
8. Business cards
9. Car keys
10. Cassette tape
11. Coin-operated arcades
12. Classified ads
13. Dial-up internet access
14. DVD player
15. Encyclopedia
16. Fax machine
17. Film rolls
18. Floppy disk
19. Incandescent light bulb
20. Key punch cards
21. Matchmakers
22. Milkman
23. Movie rental stores
24. Office binders
25. Pager
26. Paid pornography *(Playboy)*
27. Payphones
28. PDAs *(personal digital assistants)*
29. Personal checks
30. Pinball machines
31. Phone book
32. Polaroid photo
33. Printed road maps
34. Property rental agents
35. Record stores
36. Small portable TVs
37. Smoking in bars
38. Stamps
39. Stand-alone GPS units in cars
40. Stand-alone bowling alleys
41. Subway tokens
42. Telemarketing
43. Travel agency shops
44. Typewriter
45. TV news
46. VHS tapes
47. VCR player
48. Walkman
49. Wall telephones
50. Yellow pages

FOLLOW THE MONEY

Industries & jobs of the future

Here you find a selection of the 30+ billion dollar industries of the future — assembled by **Compassion in Politics**.

Future billion dollar industries

Mobile payments

Social e-commerce

Mobile health care

Government data transparency

Green data about supply chains

Online *(drone)* delivery

Mobile education

Self-coaching

Digital lifestyle design

Mass automation in human resources

Build your own dashboard *(DIY data)*

Health Informatics

If you are not already in one of them, try to link in with these future industries.

Jobs of the future

As industries are transforming *(blurring, fading and expanding)* we see totally new roles appear. Think of new jobs such as: Telesurgeon, Garbage Designer, Body Part Maker, Nostalgist, Healthcare Navigator, Time Broker, Gamification Designer, ideaDJ, Robot Counsellor, etc.

"We are preparing students for jobs that do not exist yet."

— *Sir Ken Robinson*

surface web

the deep web

3 tips for an innovative web search

1. Proper off-line preparation

You shouldn't just start a Google search.
Imagine your answer! Start by meticulously
writing down your conditions for a query
— for instance:

- What does the ideal answer look like?
  Use this exact same wording as a
  search query: imagine the ideal page
  answering your queries.

- What are the five to seven essential
  terms in my query?

2. Solo brainstorming

By now, you have settled into your query. Take time to gain some perspective. After all, you're looking for something still unknown to you. So, you can't realistically expect to find an answer via Google as you do not have the right search term yet. Therefore, it is best to imagine the cases you might find on the net.

Come up with a list of over fifty new product, service or process ideas around your query. The weirder, the better. Subsequently, run a search on the net for these imaginary products. You'll automatically end up on websites you wouldn't usually find.

3. Deep web search

A great deal of information is not directly accessible via Google. Many diverse sources — large databases, libraries and archives — have to be queried directly. That's why you need to use Google to scout out your main sources and then — one by one — research these sources using the query tools provided.

At a certain point it's time to leave Google — as Google only offers us a fraction of the Internet. An good starting point is **www.info.com** — where you can search over multiple search engines.

Google like a pro

Cross-industry search tips. Let's test and try a more advanced search with Google.

Google

```
|
```

Google Search   **I'm Feeling Lucky**

SETTINGS > ADVANCED SEARCH

GOOGLE ADVANCED SEARCH

Use the following search operators to enhance your search outcomes:

FIND EXACT

REMOVE WORDS

CONNECT WORDS

SEARCH IN A SITE

SEARCH LINKED SITES

TIME, DATE, PRICE RANGE

SIMILAR SITES

Find your list

Use logical numbers to pinpoint actual lists:

"10 trends" automotive

"top 50 innovative companies"

"top 100 innovations"

Look into the future

Use round numbers and ask for future:

Automotive in 2025

Retail in 2050

Future of transport

The power of the asterisk*

Try the '*', the wildcard and joker. The asterisk is not so commonly used in searches — yet it is a very powerful method to get nice results when you search for parts of search terms.

*"top * food trends"*

you will get 'top 5', 'top 7', 'top100', etc.

*"disrupt the * industry"*

you will find disrupting innovations.

Search in other sources

Look in: SlideShare, YouTube, Prezi, LinkedIn, Facebook, Wordpress, etc.

There's an app for that

There might already be an app specific around the theme you are looking for. Visit the App or Play Store.

Find your Twitter experts

Use the advanced search option on Twitter to find the most influential innovators regarding your search question.

And finally …
how to find 'lost' websites

The internet archive is a fantastic website which takes *screenshots* of websites with certain intervals — look back in the past:

www.archive.org

inspiring industries & smart sectors

New industries start with people having fun.

— *Tim O'Reilly*

Inspiring industries & smart sectors

Cross-industry inspiration can be found at different levels.

In the next three chapters we zoom in on 3 levels at which you can draw cross-industry inspiration:

Chapter 4 – industry / sector:
   Inspiring industries & smart sectors
Chapter 5 – company / organisation:
   WWxD? — What Would x Do?
Chapter 6 – product / service / process:
   Your business challenges

Starting up new ideas, new solutions and new industries

Start-ups sometimes create totally new industries and define new ways of working. In the process, they also develop new language. Many start-ups apply the concept – combine – create principle to come up with new solutions, new sectors and new words. Think of: Hackathon, A / B testing, Angel Investor, Minimal Viable Product, Monetisation, Pivot, User Experience Design, etc.

The IT and high- and biotech industries are currently famous for and seen as drivers of growth and innovation — yet there are so many more inspiring industries to learn from. Let's take a look.

The art of war

War and human conflict have always been a source of misery. At the same time, one cannot deny that they have also been incredible drivers for innovation.

You might be surprised by the long list of military inventions that have been integrated into everyday use. Our inability to live in peace has brought us inventions such as satellites, GPS, duct tape, microwaves, digital cameras, plastic surgery, night vision, canned food, and even nylon stockings — as a replacement for silk due to a supply cut-off in WO II.

"The best military invention — from a cross-industry innovation perspective — is definitely the internet, the ultimate cross-industry connection tool!"

Uses of military inspiration:

- **Camouflage** for telecommunications: telephone poles are disguised as trees to not disturb the landscape.
- **Boot camp** in Human Resources: thorough and structural training to really get new people *on board* quickly.
- **Air Carrier** in the Travel & Leisure: a Chinese hotel chain retrofitted an old Soviet Air Carrier as a luxury hotel.

Look at the following items from the military and see how you can use these as a metaphor for your challenges:
Commando teams, Laser guidance, Communications officer, Ranks, Boot Camp, Drills, Exoskeletons, Military intelligence, Air carriers, AWACS, Tactics, Super soldiers, etc.

Let's use copy – adapt – paste to apply military tactics in your sector.

A fast formula

In the automotive sector, innovation and car design is clearly inspired by the Formula 1. By pushing the limits in racing, real breakthrough innovations are made, which then make their way to normal *(automotive)* life.

Lessons about training & control from Formula 1

Pit stop
A 5-second pit stop is the result of countless hours *(days)* of training and rehearsal. Some examples of areas in which the pit stop model is used are:

- Machine maintenance in factories
- Rehearsal for Broadway shows
- Fast food drive-throughs

Dashboard
The **Formula 1** steering wheel *(the ultimate control and feedback centre)* also acts as fully-fledged dashboard with tactile feedback; all crucial information literally at your fingertips.

More different dashboard usages:

- Crisis command centres and remote and intelligent security camera surveillance rooms
- Your smartphone settings screen
- The **Google AdWords** control panel *(marketing campaign management)*

That's all cool, yet your own car might actually be more advanced
There is every chance that a typical mass-market car will be more advanced — at least in some ways — than the average Formula 1 race car. Traction control, stability control, anti-lock brakes and adjustable suspension are all common on road cars but have been banned from Formula 1 for years.

Check your *(Formula 1)* **car for inspiration!**

Let your ideas take flight

Air travel has always appealed to dreams and innovation. From the ultimate dream of being able to fly to a commodity, from transportation to retail.

The airline industry has inspired many crossovers. Let's take a look at a few examples.

How landing gear inspired a baby stroller

Using the concept of an airplane's retractable landing gear, **Owen Maclaren** — a retired aeronautical engineer and test pilot who worked on the Spitfire — developed the first foldable lightweight baby buggy, to save his daughter the struggle with her cumbersome stroller when getting in an out of airplanes. Millions of people have been using the foldable buggy ever since.

Airlines are about connections

KLM came up with the *Meet & Seat* concept, to allow people *(via opt-in)* to connect with fellow travellers based on their social media profile.

Delta teamed up with LinkedIn to offer *Innovation Class tickets* with which LinkedIn members had the opportunity to meet and fly with select industry leaders on a designated Delta flight.

Let your ideas take flight and think of:

Air traffic control centre, Artificial horizon, Air miles, Black box, Baggage belt, Call sign, Check check double check, Ground crew, Hangar, Hub, Payload, Sidewinder, Slipstream, Transponder, Ultralight, Flight simulator, Fail-safe, Parachute, Ground visibility, First-class lounge, Retina scan, Unmanned flight, Drone, Airborne retail, Mayday, Frequent flyer, etc.

Check, check, double check

Hospitals could also take a queue from air travel.

Crew... prepare for safety!

The Belgian hospital **AZ Sint-Maarten** in Mechelen was looking for a pleasant way to make the doctors and nurses in operating rooms more aware of safety procedures. They found their inspiration in the airline business.

Safety checklists and the airplane maintenance double check system, in which mechanics and pilots check each other's work — constitute a normal routine for airliners — but at that time it was still new for hospital operating rooms.

The hospital reached out to **Rudy Pont** — flight safety officer at Thomas Cook — and asked him to help them learn from airline safety procedures. This led to the making of a video in which a medical team runs through the safe surgery checklist as if they were an aircraft crew.

The video was shown during a big event at the hospital, increasing awareness and enabling employees to look at safety in a new and refreshing manner.

How might you use cross-industry experiences to boost your message?

Fast fashion & futuristic fabrics

It's fashionable to be futuristic. Fashion is one of the greatest ways to express oneself.

Fast fashion

Fast Fashion is the principle for stores such as **Zara** to produce catwalk-inspired collections in the shortest time frame possible at low costs to capture the latest trends.

Milk anyone?

Biologist and designer **Anke Domaske** created a natural fibre from milk for use in textiles that is water-resistant and tear-proof and the best news… the new fabric *(Qmilch)* is anti-allergenic.

As more people are reacting badly to the chemicals they encounter in daily life — from clothing to bedding or even car seats — there is a great interest in natural milk fibres from automobile manufacturers, hotels and medical technicians, as they wish to apply these materials.

Techno fashion and wearables

Fashion technology enables: size-adjustable, instantly dry, self-cleaning, colour-changing and even body temperature-balancing clothing.

Another one bites the dust

Desso carpets — with its circular economic model shaped around *Cradle to Cradle* design principles — came up with a carpet *(AirMaster)* that traps and contains dust particles until it is time to vacuum clean again.

Combine fashionable concepts with your business:

Fashionista, Style guide, Fashion blog, Beauty contest, Youtube make-up movement, Intelligent textiles, Suit, Runway, Haute couture, Confection, Recessionista, Catwalk, Fashion tribes, Connected clothing, Fast fashion, Fashion statement, Mannequin, Swag, Supermodel, etc.

Go go! Lady Gaga!

Jamie Anderson, Jörg Reckhenrich and Martin Kupp **did some cool research on a great subject to learn from: Lady Gaga.**

Remixing the music business

Lady Gaga shows how an individual *(or organisation)* can shake up an established industry merely by framing and answering differently to fundamental strategic questions, like *"Who is my customer?"*, *"What do I offer my customer?"* and *"How do I create value for my customer and ultimately myself?"*

The researchers discovered 4 key lessons businesses can learn from Lady Gaga.

Excellence

Combining her classical music background with the guts to try new things, hence providing true unique performances.

Empathy

Building emotional ties with her audience: they see her as a *friend* and most people decide to buy her music instead of illegally downloading it.

Exclusivity

Informing her fans — her *little monsters* — even before the media, hence building a unique relationship.

eCommerce

Working with a new business model *the 360 deal* where music companies actually take a stake in the artist business *(more like venture capital)* opposed to traditional record label contracts.

Can you Gaga your strategy?

Shoot for the moon!

When children are asked what they want to be when they grow up, astronaut makes third place on their wish list *(preceded only by secret agents and superheroes)*.

It's clear that aerospace powers imagination from an early age. How could it not? Space travel itself is literally crossing borders into the big unknown.

"There's more space in your life than you think."

Bringing space technology down to earth

The inventions made for space have been put to good use in our earthly realms as well. **NASA**'s liquid-cooled space clothing — for example — worn by lunar astronauts, has been adapted to help burn victims. The space agency also helped develop a lightweight breathing system for fire fighters.

"When we design an X Prize our mission is to launch an industry, not to reward a historic moment."

— *Peter Diamandis*

Other things we can thank this industry for are water filters, scratch-resistant lenses, memory foam mattresses, baby food, space blankets, CMOS sensors for phone cameras, LEDs, the joystick and even a perfume called *Zen* from a rose grown in space. Recently — biologists modified the star-tracking algorithms used by the Hubble Telescope to track fish, polar bears and even terrorists.

NASA's Technology Transfer Program aims to bring NASA technology to businesses via licensing models. NASA lists over 1,800 technologies on their website — that made it from space back to earth.

Are you ready to use 'out of this world' insights for your business?

Think of: Mission control, Capsules, Satellites, Aliens, Launch pads, Lift-off, Orbit, Re-entry, Touch down, X Prize, Spacewalk, Zero gravity, Virgin galactic, Atmosphere, *Beam me up Scotty*, Research stations and the Moonwalk!

TOOL

Business synonyms

Business synonyms

Using different viewpoints is a great way to go cross-industry. If you've ever flown via Heathrow Airport — you've probably spotted the beautiful ads from **HSBC** — The Hong Kong Shanghai Banking Corporation — in which they focus on cross-cultural understanding as they give different meanings to different words.

We take this a step further with our **Business Synonyms Method**. Use our method to help you look for other industries in which they deal differently with your situation.

Steps:

1. Keep your situation in mind.
2. Select the **business synonym** which addresses a key element of your situation.
3. Go through the list of words, say them out loud.
4. Wait for the concept that leaps out for you.
5. Apply that insight!

Customer = Client = Consumer = Student = Patient = Shopper = Buyer = Purchaser = End-user = Patron = Prospect = Supplier = Pain in the *ss = King = Queen = Dancer = Singer = Guest = Troublemaker = Boss = Employee = Stakeholder = Civilian = Savage = Animal = Child = Teacher = Necessity = A means to an aim = Lifesaver = Relation = Keeper = Renter = Leaser = Holder = Occupant = Vacationer = Visitor = Caller = Tenant = Tourist = Foreigner = Alien = Citizen = Native = Traveller = User = Window shopper = Collector = Associate = Business partner = Competitor = ...

Service = Help = Support = Listening = Aid = Life Support = Account = Advantage = Applicability = Appropriateness = Assistance = Avail = Benefit = Business = Check = Courtesy = Dispensation = Duty = Employ = Employment = Favour = Fitness = Indulgence = Kindness = Labour = Maintenance = Ministration = Office = Overhaul = Relevance = Serviceability = Servicing = Supply = Use = Usefulness = Utility = Value = Work = Care = Treatment = Comfort = Giving = Responsibility = Facilitation = Sustenance = Participation = Communication = Doing business with = Give-and-take = Helpfulness = ...

Sales = Transaction = Delivery = Promise = Relief = Wonder = Success = Dream come true = Story = Transfer = Auction = Business = Buying = Trade = Deal = Demand = Marketing = Merchandising = Vending machine = Acquiring = Commercialism = Free market = Game = Bargaining = Distribution = Exchange = Undertaking = Handover = Peacocking = Advertising = Free samples = Call to action = Persuasion = Contracts = Win-win = Capitalizing = Competition = Agreement = Consensus = Cooperation = Harmony = Highest bid = Sell-out = Sell-off = Offering = Negotiation = Pull = Retail = Wholesale = Sweet talk = Hustle = Growth = Close the deal = ...

Supply chain = Handover = Flow = Transfer = Process = Column = Chain = Tube = Method = Series of actions to achieve result = Action = Advance = Case = Channels = Course = Course of action = Development = Evolution = Fashion = Formation = Growth = Manner = Means = Measure = Food chain = Mechanism = Mode = Modus operandi = Movement = Transaction = Operation = Outgrowth = Performance = Practice = Procedure = Proceeding = Progress = Progression = Red tape = Routine = Rule = Stage = Step = Suit = System = Technique = Trial = Unfolding = Way = ...

TOOL

Business synonyms

Steps:

1. Keep your situation in mind.
2. Select the **business synonym** which addresses a key element of your situation.
3. Go through the list of words, say them out loud.
4. Wait for the concept that leaps out for you.
5. Apply that insight!

Costs = Investment = Fee = Tuition = Price = Prize = Amount = Charge = Toll = Dues = Rate = Payment = Value = Squeeze = Ticket = Expenditure = Damage = Worth = Restitution = Penalty = Debt = Premium = Wage = Pay-off = Bill = Expense = Quota = Percentage = Bad news = Misfortune = Unexpected = Margin = Bottom dollar = Wallet = Draining = Cash flow = Capital = Split = Asset = Credit = Loan = Payback = Savings = Bank account = Budget = Funds = Resources = Spending = Means = Finances = ...

Reduction = Less = Percentage = Fee = Contraction = Cut = Cutback = Devaluation = Discount = Downgrading = Decrement = Degradation = Minimization = Shrinkage = Subtraction = Synopsis = Summary = Sketch = Compression = Narrowing = Tightening = Deflating =Recession = Loss = Downturn = Decline = Drop = Fall = Decay = Weakening = Deterioration = Failing = Drawback = Roll-back = Knock-off = Markdown = Bargain = Ebb = Depression = In a nutshell = Small = Tapered = Chopped = Trim = Diminish = Restricted = Clipped = Abbreviated = Lightened = Essence = ...

WWxD?
What Would
x Do?

WWXD?

What Would x Do?

In this chapter we investigate how other companies tackle their business challenges and what you can learn from them.

By no means can we be comprehensive, as we could easily write an entire book *(in some cases multiple)* per company on lessons to learn from them. We have chosen a few well-known companies and hope to offer a few, perhaps lesser known insights.

Keep in mind that cross-industry innovation analogies can be drawn at various levels: from products to services, to processes, to strategies, to leadership styles, to business models.

Now ask yourself: What Would x Do?

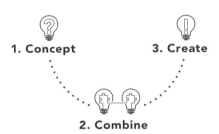

1. Concept

2. Combine

3. Create

Serious Play

The ultimate combination tool is of course LEGO.

The LEGO company has witnessed highs and lows in terms of business operations. The key is to find the essential building blocks that make LEGO successful and discover how you can apply these to your situation. Keep in mind: Lego is not just a toy — it's a whole industry.

Here are 5 business lessons we can learn from LEGO:

1. From the beginning — LEGO was designed to be modular and compatible with older bricks.

2. LEGO is unafraid to experiment with emerging new technologies to extend its brand reach from physical to digital play.

3. LEGO gives its designers cost parameters: they can design anything they want as long as it falls within budget. These cost limitations resulted in a spike of creativity.

4. LEGO is not *(just)* for children. LEGO focuses on completely new target groups, such as:

Business
    LEGO Serious Play certified managers
Hobby
    Adult Fan of LEGO networks
Entertainment
    The LEGO Movie

5. LEGO combines different types of innovation. LEGO does not just engage in product innovation, but also plays with components such as: network, process, product system, brand and channels.

What components in your business can you play with?

Radical retail

In his research for the book *The Apple Experience*, writer Carmine Gallo discovered ten things that the Apple Store can teach any business in any industry in order to be more successful.

We highlight 5 things you can learn from the Apple Store here:

Stop selling stuff

Don't ask *"How will we grow our market share?"* instead — ask *"How do we enrich people's lives?"*.

Celebrate diversity

Tattoos, piercings and crazy hair styles are all acceptable among Apple Store employees; they are selected to reflect the diversity of their customers.

Empower employees

Apple has a non-commissioned sales floor for a reason. Employees are not pressured to make a sale.

Sell the benefit

Apple Store specialists are taught to sell the benefit behind products and to customise those benefits for the customer.

Create multi-sensory experiences

Every device in an Apple Store is working and connected to the Internet. Customers are invited to play — the sense of touch helps create an emotional connection with a product.

Angela Ahrendts — the successful former CEO of Burberry — became the Senior Vice President of Retail and Online Sales for Apple, a clear cross-sector hire to enhance Apple retail even more.

I mean Picasso
had a saying:

good artists copy,
great artists steal.

And we have always been shameless about stealing great ideas.

And I think part of what made the Macintosh great, was that the people working on it were musicians and poets and artists and zoologists and historians who also happened to be the best computer scientists in the world. — *Steve Jobs*

In search of sectors

Google wants to make all information in the world available to everybody. This concept radically transforms industries that are based on closed information systems and monopoly.

Google crosses industries continuously

Google started out as a search engine — yet ended up making an incredible amount of crossovers.

Year	Sector	Product
1998:	web	Search
2000:	advertising	AdWords
2002:	news	News
2004:	e-mail	Gmail
2005:	geo	Maps
2006:	video	YouTube
2006:	office	Docs
2008:	mobile	Android
2011:	money	Wallet
2012:	life	Now
2013:	things	Glass
2014:	automotive	Self-driving cars

Googlify your business

Floating energy?

Did you know Google is one of the largest energy producers in the world? With even their own energy plants? In addition — there are Google's floating data-centres — which are connected containers in the sea that house some of the vast number of Google servers. Their containers generate power from the movement of the sea and also directly use the sea water for cooling.

WWGD?

What Would Google Do? — is a great book by **Jeff Jarvis**. Filled with insights on the way Google operates, how Google makes money, in which segments Google is active and what Google would do if they would enter other industries. A good and recommended read after *Not Invented Here*.

Google's Mission Statement is:

"To organize the world's information and make it universally accessible and useful."

Review your mission statement and check for combinations with unusual sectors.

Construct your own crossovers

A few examples of IKEA's unique naming scheme:

Fabrics, curtains – *Women's names*

Garden furniture – *Swedish islands*

Carpets – *Danish place names*

Beds, wardrobes, hallway furniture – *Norwegian place names*

Dining tables and chairs – *Finnish place names*

Bookcase ranges – *Occupations*

Bathroom articles – *Scandinavian lakes, rivers and bays*

Cool facts about IKEA that can inspire your company

Product naming *(instead of numbering)*
IKEA products have Scandinavian-sounding names rather than numbers, because the founder mr. Kamprad is dyslexic.

Living diversity
IKEA was the first company to feature a portrayal of a gay relationship in one of its ads.

Loveable marketing
Each year, more copies are printed of the catalogue than of the Bible. It's not just a catalogue; it's more like a coffee table photo book.

Management by walking around
IKEA managers walk around the stores and parking places on a structural basis — asking customers whether they need any help *(e.g. with loading their cars)* and inquiring into their level of satisfaction.

Geo marketing
Everybody within a 45-minute drive from an IKEA store receives a catalogue at their home address. Anyone living outside that zone … is just too far out!

Walk your talk
Its super rich founder — *Ingvar Kamprad* — is frugal with his spendings.

Smart routing
IKEA stores have a predetermined walking route — yet it includes smart shortcuts for people who want to be fast.

Portability
Most IKEA products have been designed to be transported in flat packs.

Product extension
IKEA is now selling entire prefab homes named *BoKlok*.

An integrated business (machine)

IBM — international business machines — is a pretty unique and complex organisation. If you're looking for some next practices in management and organisation, IBM is actually a great resource.

For instance — to become an IBM global leader — you need to have worked in at least 3 continents. This is to ensure that you have a *global view*.

In addition, IBM is an early example of a matrix organisation, which tries to deliver expertise on the full grid of the matrix. In some cases, IBM is organising it's own competition — different departments go after the same client projects — coining the motto:

"It's better to disrupt yourself than let someone else do it."

Who says elephants can't dance?

Who says elephants can't dance? is a good book on organisational change and playing with components, written by **Lou Gerstner** *(ex IBM CEO)* on his transformation of IBM.

The major change Gerstner made — and the one he himself is most proud of — was to stop a plan well underway in order to divide IBM into different operating entities. Gerstner saw that only an integrated approach *(Hardware, Software and Services)* would enable IBM to deliver complete solutions to its clients. A clear case of organised cross-pollination in a very large organisation.

Under the leadership of **Sam Palmisano** and now CEO **Ginni Rometty** — IBM has moved into selling most of the hardware parts and made the shift from being a service provider to a solutions integrator. That integration clearly takes place at the edge of industries, where they are able to link everything together.

———

How might you become a more integrated business machine?

Mazda, Netflix, General Electric, Aldi, Cirque du Soleil, Virgin, IKEA, Amazon, Toyota, Disneyland, Siemens, Airbnb, Coca-Cola, PayPal, Red Bull, Intel, LinkedIn, DHL, Twitter, Tesco, eBay, Gillette, HP, Zara, Starbucks, Visa, Google, Verizon, IBM, Google, Uber, Pizzahut, Harley Davidson, XIAOMI, Dropbox, Nike, Yelp, Tesla Motors, WhatsApp, Baidu, Tencent, LEGO, Shazam, Nest, Dyson, Bitcoin, Sony, Watergen, Unicef, Spotify, YouTube, Moleskine, Solarcity, NASA, Boeing, Lego, Unilever, Tupperware, KLM, Bic, Navy Seals, Target, Fisher-Prise, 3M, Chiquita, Kodak, Volkswagen, Rolex, Microsoft, MTV, American Airlines, Warner Bros, Levi's, Ford, Alibaba, Pixar, Harrods, etc.

WWxD?

Do It Yourself: What Would x Do?

You can start by asking *WWxD?* and look for inspiring principles or learnings to fertilise your own business. For instance:

"What would Alibaba do if it bought your company?"

Be specific

An even smarter approach is to focus on a specific element of your example company 'x'.

Always look for at least 5 things the specific 'x' does:

1. differently
2. strangely
3. remarkably
4. out of the ordinary
5. not do… *(what they don't do)*

Let's check out this example for BMW:

Product	*What would the BMW i8 electric car sales team do?*
Service	*What would the BMW concierge service operators do?*
Process	*What would the BMW head of logistical planning do?*
Technology	*What would the BMW engine design team do?*
Business model	*What would the BMW leasing team do?*
Strategy	*What would the BMW supervisory board do?*

Cross-industry transfer map

Steps

1. Think of an inspiring organisation and write down the name *(or draw the logo)*.
2. List the key properties of WHAT they do and HOW they do it *(write on Post-its)*.
3. Select certain practices *(Post-its)* and transfer them to your situation, ask yourself:
   "How might we apply these insights?"

• • • **Inspiring company, organisation:** • • •

WHAT CAN WE LEARN FROM THIS ORGANISATION?

1. Concept

2. C

·>

·>

Our situation:

**HOW MIGHT WE APPLY THESE
LESSONS TO OUR SITUATION?**

·>

e

3. Create

your business challenges

When was the last time ...

... you did something for the first time?

Your business challenges

Cross-industry innovation can be described as a profitable meeting of contexts, where previously there was no connection.

Arthur Koestler — a pioneer of creative thinking — describes creativity as the collision of two apparently unrelated frames of reference.

Across various industries — many organisations struggle with the same issues and actually have common challenges that are not always recognised as similar.

In this chapter we'll focus on a few key challenges many organisations face:

- Boosting customer value
- Growing your business
- Becoming a greener business
- Taking care of elegant cost-cutting
- Supercharging your supply chain
- Combine for more value
- Changing behaviour
- Generate more impact

It's time for something new because:

"When you do what you always did, you will get what you always got."

Let's learn from others how they tackle similar business challenges.

How do other industries
generate more value?

customer
value

company
customer

commodities · products · services · solutions · experience · engagement

level of customer

You can increase value for your customers, your company and the world by making the following jumps:

Commodities	→	Products
Products	→	Services
Services	→	Solutions
Solutions	→	Experience
Experience	→	Engagement
Engagement	→	… ?

Look at other companies and sectors that have made jumps already, like the leisure industry — hotels, cruises and adventure travelling — and retail — flagship stores of international brands, fun shopping and pop-up shops.

At each jump, the customer interaction increases and you are actually creating a fan base, which clearly also increases the value for the company.

The rebellious Belgian Telecom operator **Mobile Vikings** has the slogan:

"Mobile internet and free communication among all Vikings."

This creates a very strong community of customers who see themselves as Vikings and actively attract new Vikings.

———

Make a list of 3 of your favourite companies or organisations where you as customer clearly come first, really experience the brand, and are engaged. Find out why and which principles you can use for your own company.

Grow your business!

How to attract more clients?
How to drive revenue?
How to boost sales?

Learn from these 6 smart examples:

Simplify

Amazon was the first website to offer *one-click* orders. How might you simplify your sales process?

Cut the crap

Some customers are looking for cheap, no frills products or services. Think of low-cost airlines and Lidl supermarkets. Can you think of a low-budget version of your business?

Virtual buying

Make it possible to buy everywhere. For instance, the Tesco virtual supermarket in the Seoul subway consists of life-sized billboards that look like real supermarket shelves, where each product is displayed with a QR code. After each mobile transaction, the products are delivered to your home.

Try before you buy

Let customers test or try out your product. Why can you easily test-drive a car — yet not *test-sleep* a house you want to buy?

Freemium

Offer a basic version for free that can be upgraded. Examples: LinkedIn, Skype, consultant intakes, etc.

Aim high

Learn from luxury hotels. The Four Seasons hotels never lowers their service level not even in economic downturns, a clear long-term vision.

———

What can you learn from these *Best Selling Products of All Time*: The Toyota Corolla, Harry Potter books, PlayStation game consoles, Star Wars movies, iPad, and the Rubik's cube.

Become a greener business

6 unconventional ways to become a more sustainable business

Access is becoming more important than ownership

Use it, don't own it. Examples: textbook rentals, bike sharing and streaming music.

Integration

Many devices can do multiple things now. Think of your smart phone which doubles as: camera, calculator, music player, radio, TV, phone, address book, flashlight, alarm clock, etc.

Creative reuse

The practice of reuse isn't new, think of **Replate**: sharing your leftovers with the homeless. Another example of reuse is the **Good Bag** *(Goedzak in Dutch)*: a semi-transparent garbage bag that invites passersby to look inside and decide whether they could make use of its contents. If the goods are not taken — the bag is picked up by the waste disposal service.

Love local

Local production and consumption. An example is **Urban Farming** — which encourages people to grow their own vegetables. Another example is **CouchSurfing** — which allows you to bypass the typical hotel experience by staying at the home of a local for free and learning about their culture.

The power of zero

Zero is becoming increasingly important. Some examples: zero-energy buildings, zero waste, zero emission and zero defects.

Feedback

To increase awareness, feedback is essential. Some systems have feedback integrated, for instance the NEST learning thermostat — which directly shows your usage — and the eco-drive feature in a car, which indicates when to switch gear.

Which principles can you use for your business?

Cut costs elegantly

How to cut costs
in a smart way?

"Buurtzorg is a great example of increasing patient care and satisfaction — while also cutting costs in the process."

Buurtzorg *(neighbourhood care)* is an innovative approach in the Netherlands for providing home care. Initiated in 2006 — it originated from staff's dissatisfaction with traditional home care organisations. Bureaucratic duties — working in isolation from other care providers and, above all neglect of their professional competencies — were among the complaints.

The organisational model of Buurtzorg is to have care provided by small self-managing teams consisting of a maximum of twelve professional caregivers. In addition — Buurtzorg wishes to keep organisational costs as low as possible, partially by using ICT to organise and register care programs.

At this moment — more than 500 self-managing teams *(6,000 caregivers)* are already operational and the company has already won the nomination for *Best company to work for* twice in the previous years.

Some additional principles and examples from various industries will help you cut your costs in an elegant manner:

Replace your most costly component: Intel Celeron Processors, Palm Oil, etc.
Multi-skilled crews: Submarine Crews, One-man TV teams, etc.
Let customers work for you (DIY): Self-service Check-in, Self-assembly Furniture, etc.

Supercharge your supply chain

If you are waiting for a sign, this is it

Sometimes things can be so easy. The **IKEA's** floor arrows are now used in many government buildings and even train stations to provide people with clear and direct guidance where they need to go.

Who's been voted the best company in supply chain operations worldwide by Gartner Research for 4 years in a row already? Nope — it's not UPS, TNT or Amazon… It's Apple.

The promise that a new computer or iPhone is available *today* is even more magical than Apple's impressive marketing of the devices. Standardisation of Apple's product offerings and streamlining supply chain operations, was key to achieving this logistical masterpiece.

Go with the flow.
From container belts to containers, to…

After the conveyer belt — one of the greatest impacts on supply chain management was the container. This incredible standardisation has helped optimise logistics dramatically.

Now it's time for the next jump in supply chain operations: the self-driving container truck. The Rotterdam harbour has announced that they plan to start using their self-driving trucks outside their own grounds before 2020, making use of the technology for Google's self-driving car concept. This is no longer science fiction.

Imagine the impact of self-driving trucks. We'll have less traffic jams because trucks will *know* what to do; no mandatory breaks for resting; no more parking issues — as the truck will drive away and come back when it's needed; very efficient logistics — as the truck can be used in a *meta pool*.

How could you guide people effortlessly through your organisation?
Can you standardise something no-one has ever thought of?
What can you make self-operating?

Combine for more value

Back in 1928, **Fiat Lingotto** found alternative usage for their rooftop. They installed a racetrack on the rooftop of the factory so that cars could be tested on site.

The Dutch cooperation **Dakwaarde** *(roof value)* keeps an up-to-date overview of thousands of examples on what else you can do with your roof:
www.pinterest.com/dakwaarde

What else can you use your rooftop for?

- Solar panels
- Small wind energy mills
- Roof gardens
- Food roofs *(farming)*
- Sport fields

Other examples of added value by combining functions

Social care farm – combines working farms with care needs. **Water basin square** – is a public space that can hold mud water in case of flooding. **Solar roadways** – where special tarmac is used as solar panels. **Smart street sweeper** – a street sweeper car that can be converted to a snow remover vehicle in winter.

Try to think of which functions you could combine for more value?

Change behaviour

Can we get more people to observe the speed limit by making it fun to do?

The speed camera lottery

A test in Copenhagen *(Denmark)* with the speed camera lottery proved that fun really can change behaviour.

What they did was simple: on a selected route in the city — all drivers got their speed measured and photographed. The people speeding got a fine and the people who kept to the speed limit were entered into a lottery for the collective money paid by the people who had been caught speeding.

This resulted in a 22% drop of the average speed. A great result! The initiative that collects these ideas is called The Fun Theory — powered by Volkswagen.

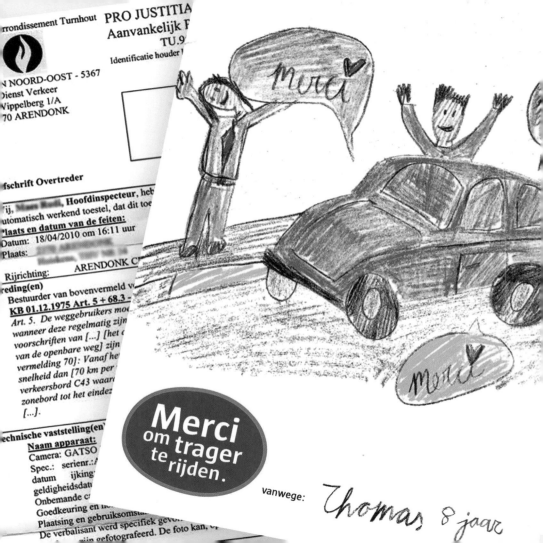

Generate more impact

Use the element of surprise and make your message go viral.

Thank you for not speeding

Road users caught speeding in Antwerp receive a ticket and a child's drawing.

Thank you for not speeding — is the message that will appear on every drawing as part of the campaign instigated by the Antwerp police. The police asked the city's primary school pupils to send in drawings. Of the 1,150 drawings submitted — 450 made the cut and were printed. The police has sent out 30,000 drawings *(and fines)* so far.

Concert cancelled?!

The Belgian city of Ghent had a lot of trouble removing illegal adverts for parties. Finally — instead of removing the adverts or trying to hunt down the people hanging up the posters — the city council decided to have civil servants paste notifications over the posters with texts such as:

"Cancelled" or "New date"

This immediately led to a significant drop in illegal pasting of posters.

How might you surprise your customers, suppliers, civilians or partners?

21 ways cross-industry inspiration

21 ways to strategise and innovate is a set of critical questions, checklists and examples from all over the world to help you innovate.

21 ways sets provide cross-industry inspiration for: product and service ideas, product development, process and service innovations, government innovations, business model innovation new business development and defining strategic directions.

Based on a client's question, we extract important trends, successful innovations, principles or evolutions. The list of 21 principles changes per question. 21 ways sets are useful in individual or group brainstorms, in new business development and strategy sessions.

Combining the input with an interactive engaging presentation and/or workshop clearly helps to come up with new connections, great ideas and enriched concepts.

On the next page we outline a cross-industry example for you to use.

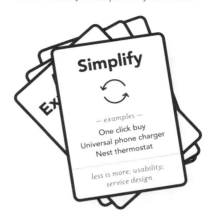

The steps for using this tool:

1. Investigate the principle: what is the essence? → CONCEPT
2. Make a direct association *(copy-paste)* for your situation → COMBINE
3. Make two conceptual associations *(copy-adapt-paste)* for your situation → COMBINE
4. What should we do or use? And how might we test this quickly? → CREATE

Visit crossindustryinnovation.com to download your own card set and see more examples of 21 ways sets.

21 ways: innovation principles

principle	examples	related principles
SHARING	BlaBlaCar / Zipcar / Sharedesk	collaborative consumption / sharing is the new buying / fractional ownership
LOW TECH SOLUTIONS	Aravind / A liter of light / One laptop per child	frugal innovation / reverse innovation / jugaad innovation
HYBRID SOLUTIONS	Hybrid cars / Solar sailor / Hybrid notebook	combination innovation / co-creation
SHORTCUTTING	Airbnb / Farm to table / Zopa	desintermediation / cut out the middleman
TRANSPARENCY	Mint (finance) / Open restaurant kitchen / Salesforce.com's Trust website	corporate governance / open data
FROM PRODUCT TO SOLUTION	Rolls-Royce power by the hour / Hilti / John Deere services	experience economy / service economy
INTERNET OF THINGS	Ninja Blocks / Smart cities / Mimo baby monitor	cloud of things / smart networked objects
BIG DATA	Patientslikeme / Twitter / Facebook	internet of things / business model innovation
PEER TO PEER	Zopa / Gidsy / Uber / SideShare	shortcutting / crowdsourcing
DIGITISATION	Wikipedia / Netflix / Dropbox	lean / e-commerce

principle	examples	related principles
SIMPLIFY	Nest thermostat / One click buy / Universal phone charger	less is more / service design
ADD EXPERIENCE	Starbucks / Walt Disney / Red Bull	experience economy / exclusivity
CO-BRANDING	Nike + iPod / Senseo / Heinz / Lays ketchup chips	co-creation / brand alliances
LOW COST	Easy group / H&M / Ryanair	business model / frugal innovation
GO GREEN	Solar road / Eco font / Zero energy home	eco-innovation / circular economy
MASS CUSTOMISATION	Nike ID / My M&M's / Unique bag	personalisation / 3D printing
COMMUNITY BUILDING	Harley Davidson / Apple	consumer tribes / personal branding
STORYTELLING	Ben & Jerry's / KFC / Facebook	authenticity / roots
CUSTOMER IN CONTROL	Fixmystreet / Parcel tracking information / LEGO digital designer	prosumers / co-creation
DO IT YOURSELF	Ikea / Self check-in / Employee self service	self-service / lean
CROWDSOURCING	TomTom Map Share / Kickstarter / Open source software	crowdfunding / open innovation

CHAPTER

the power of
the unexpected

**WHERE
THE MAGIC
HAPPENS**

**YOUR
COMFORT
ZONE**

The power of the unexpected

For cross-industry innovation you also need to embrace the power of the unexpected to create something new.

Superhero window cleaning

Young patients at the Children's Hospital in Minneapolis *(USA)* got a surprise when they looked out the window. Batman, Superman and Spiderman took a break from their normal superhero duties to wash the windows at the hospital.

"Inspiration can come from everything, if not... look again."
— *Paul Arden*

In this chapter we will learn from some very unexpected places. Let's take a look at arts, nature, festivals, fun, history and even organised crime.

Heatwave
your product

This is the heatwave radiator designed by Joris Laarman for Jaga.

The heatwave is a true piece of art that doubles as a radiator. This modular heating system can even be extended to bend around a corner.

In addition to being a popular radiator, several museums — from Paris to New York — have taken up the heatwave in their collection.

There are many more examples for which art has been used to enhance and enrich common products and services.

How might we draw inspiration from the artist who decided to print the London metro map on a bracelet and thereby created a functional piece of jewellery?

Or think of **Allessi**; a brand that understands the art of upgrading household appliances by means of design very well. Remember the *Birillio*? This artful product pushed the sales price of a toilet brush up by 800%. Another example is those complex and boring data made user-friendly through infographics created by great designers.

Art spans many areas — so when you're looking to use art to enhance your product or service — don't forget about street art, musicians, cartoonists, installation artists, performance art, photography, graffiti, life art, crowd-sourced art, fashion art, audiovisual art and many more.

How might you tap into the arts to boost your product or service?

Turn location data into beautiful jewellery

Meshu.io has found a really cool way to use art to generate stylish impact. By plotting various locations on a map you can create a true personalised piece of jewellery or print.

Alternative uses for this concept are:
- All the places you did events for a client
- The locations of your company
- The places where someone has been stationed during their career
- All the places parcels were before delivery
- ...

Here's how it works:

Enter in cities you've been to, or any places you like.

Meshu creates a necklace, earrings, ring, or a print.

Meshu fabricates and ships your finished piece to wherever you want!

What can you do with 'locations or geo-data' to create impact?

Burn your business?

Every year, a temporary community comes together in the Nevada desert to celebrate creativity across boundaries.

Imagine a half moon-shaped city in the middle of the desert. Out of nowhere… where nothing is sold and 50,000 people live, share and express themselves.

This is **Burning Man**. It's called Burning Man because of the wooden man that gets burnt on the last night of the festival.

Learn from Burning Man,
which is built upon these 10 principles:
Radical inclusion – *anyone can be a part of Burning Man*
Gifting – *gifting does not require a return or an exchange*
Decommodification – *we don't do money*
Radical self-reliance – *everyone brings their own resources*
Radical self-expression – *do what you want*
Communal effort – *creative cooperation and collaboration*
Civic responsibility – *be responsible, don't hurt anybody*
Leaving no trace – *zero impact on the environment*
Participation – *everyone is invited to work and play*
Immediacy – *attention on the now*

How could you use radical principles to enable self-organisation?

Nature has 3.8 billion years of experience in creating sustainable environments, renewable structures and communication systems, so it might be a good strategy to learn from nature.

Become a natural

Innovation inspired by nature

Biomimicry is the practice of learning from nature — its models, systems and processes — in order to solve human challenges.

"Those who are inspired by a model other than Nature — a mistress above all masters — are labouring in vain."

— *Leonardo Da Vinci*

In our daily lives we encounter many innovations inspired by nature already, such as Velcro based on seed sacs of plants that cling to animal fur; new drugs based on what chimps eat when they are sick; high-speed trains that have been modelled upon the shape of a kingfisher bird; the **Speedo Fastskin** swimsuit — that mimics a shark's skin — significantly reducing water drag; and a passive cooling system based on how termite hills work.

The bionic… car!

Mercedes-Benz decided to model a concept car after a boxfish due to the minimal air resistance of its body shape and the rigidity of its exoskeleton, which influenced the car's unusual appearance. This design allowed for 80% lower nitrogen oxide emissions.

Janine Benyus — author of the great book: *Biomimicry – Innovation Inspired by Nature* — states that there are three types of biomimicry: **copying form and shape**, like the design of Velcro does; **copying a process**, such as photosynthesis in a leaf; or **mimicry at an ecosystem level**, for instance building a nature-inspired city.

How might you apply natural concepts, knowing that nature does not produce waste and that efficiency is an integral part of nature?

The principles of biomimicry

The fascination with nature is not new. Scientists, philosophers, architects and artists have for centuries explored the design and underlying mathematical principals of nature: the Fibonacci sequence, logarithmic spirals, organic design and the Golden Ratio are some of the many examples on how nature inspires human life.

"Left alone, nature is more efficient than any industrial system."

— *Jay Harmon*

The 9 principles of Biomimicry:

1. Nature runs on sunlight.
2. Nature uses only the energy it needs.
3. Nature fits form to function.
4. Nature recycles everything.
5. Nature rewards co-operation.
6. Nature banks on diversity.
7. Nature demands local expertise.
8. Nature curbs excesses from within.
9. Nature taps the power of limits.

Select one and see how you can use nature as your ultimate cross-industry inspiration source.

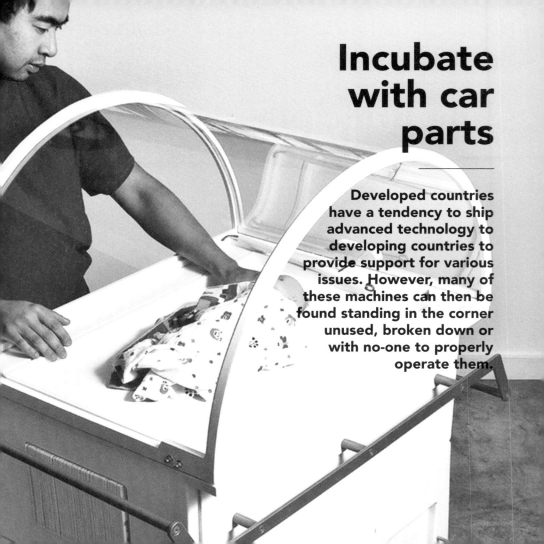

Incubate with car parts

Developed countries have a tendency to ship advanced technology to developing countries to provide support for various issues. However, many of these machines can then be found standing in the corner unused, broken down or with no-one to properly operate them.

"In Indonesia many children don't get a name until they are 2 months old. It's a cultural adaption to expect newborn death." — Dr. Kristian Olson

Keeping babies warm with a cool incubator

Dr. Jonathan Rosen was working in Indonesia and encountered the situation that many incubators were simply out of operation. While consulting with the local doctors, Dr. Rosen asked himself *"What can be repaired all over the world?"* At which point the answer struck him… cars! Toyota 4x4s, in particular. Based on this insight, Dr. Rosen worked with the company *Design that Matters* to create a new incubator created from car parts.

This is how the **NeoNurture** incubator was born. The heat source is made from a pair of headlights. A car door alarm signals emergencies. An auto air filter and fan provide climate control and a motorcycle battery and car cigarette lighter provide backup power during incubator transport and power cuts. Most car mechanics should be able to repair the NeoNurture in case it breaks down and spare parts are relatively easy to find. A truly great invention.

Frugal innovation

Frugal innovation — as described by **Carlos Ghosn**, CEO Renault–Nissan Alliance — is about doing more with less. Entrepreneurs and innovators in emerging markets have to devise low-cost strategies and overcome resource limitations to innovate.

——

Where could you use a frugal approach in your organisation?

Find inspiration in the past *(history watching)* **instead of looking for future trends** *(trendwatching)*

Many innovations containing old ideas are often not really considered all that innovative. In this respect we disagree, as there is so much to learn from concepts and ideas from the past. In fact — products, dreams, ideas and concepts from the past are a very useful source of inspiration the search for the future.

"I go to the past for research. I need to know what came before so I can break the rules." — *Vera Wang*

Let's go Back to the Future

Western Electric is crossing a telephone with a TV set.

Back to the Future tips:

Look at the future that never happened

Search for these terms to find great visual retro inspiration: Wrong predictions of the future, Paleofuture, Science Fiction, Future that never was, Retrofuturism.

Combine old and new

Consider the *new edition classics* in the automotive sector. Following the New Mini, the New Beetle and the Nuova Cinquecento — there now even is the Neue Trabi.

Counter trends

Choose to deliberately not follow the market leader and create your own counter trend. For example — **Beats by Dr. Dre**: retro-looking headphones in a stylish design and at a premium price.

Build upon ideas that didn't work (before)

You don't always need to be the first to market. The iPod wasn't the first MP3 player, Facebook wasn't the first social network and VHS won the market even though BetaMax was the established market leader.

The **Western Electric** *PicturePhone* — the predecessor of Skype, MSN Messenger and FaceTime — didn't really make it in the 50s. Today — video calling and conferencing is available to anyone with a smartphone.

Look at (your) history!

Use history watching as a new way to find future trends — take a deep dive into your own company history to find stories and *(product)* ideas you can revitalise!

Painting with Microsoft Excel

"I saw other people neatly drawing graphs — and I thought it seemed like Excel could be used to draw art."

Microsoft Excel isn't only for spreadsheets. It can also be used to create art. How? Just ask 73-year-old *Tatsuo Horiuchi*.

Digital artist

Before he retired from his company, he felt like he wanted to do something new. So he bought a computer and started using Excel. In the past ten years — he has established himself as a digital artist, showing his work at exhibitions.

Why Excel?

But why Excel? *"Other specialised graphic software is expensive, and Excel came pre-installed on PCs"* — **Horiuchi** told Japanese website PC Online — adding that he found the program easy to use and more useful than actual paint. The pensioner states that he never used Excel for his job.

What tools do you already have available that you could do alternative things with?

IT ALL STARTED WITH
A WAFFLE IRON.
Invent Better.
NIKE
BETTER
WORLD

Not-intended waffle iron use

***Bill Bowerman* — the track coach at the University of Oregon and one of Nike's founders — was constantly looking for ways to give his runners an edge.**

As he tinkered with the earliest Nike products, he sought a way to duplicate a track spike's traction with rubber.

One morning in the kitchen, he looked at his wife's waffle iron, and that's when he recognised his ultimate inspiration. The name for the new traction pattern is an elegant nod to the waffle iron: the Nike Waffle shoe was born. A clear case of *not-intended use*, yielding virtually unlimited possibilities.

"You have a wonderful lab in your home that's ideal for experimenting — it's called the kitchen." — *Chef Chris Young*

Prototyping starts at home...
What will you cook up?

Lessons from bad business & strange sectors

Take a look at these special sectors and look for three principles that make them successful. Try to adapt these principles — not necessarily the actual activities — for your organisation.

Mob
Espionage
Drug trade
Fraud squad
Gaming industry
Metro tunnelling
Hurricane hunters
Demolition industry
Underground economy
Crime scene investigation
Boeing manufacturing site
Organised crime *(syndicates)*
Polar research station construction
High-voltage power lines maintenance
Counterfeit consumer goods
Avalanche rescue teams
Submarine construction
Casino management
Lobbying industry
House movers
Porn industry
Dating sites
Mining

What we can learn from strange, uncommon or even illegal businesses?

The **Harvard Business Review** published a great article on what businesses can learn from organised crime. Here we highlight three of those business lessons.

Really jump at opportunities

Criminal groups have made an art out of scanning the environment and deploying technology at a fast rate to capitalise on what they find. Within hours of the 2010 Haiti earthquake, for example, scammers were circulating e-mails urging people to wire money to a fake account. — **Are you able to respond to opportunity faster?**

Outsource to specialists

Modern organised crime has abandoned the top-heavy structure of dons, capos, and lieutenants made famous in **The Godfather**. Most of today's gangs are loosely affiliated cooperative networks. They routinely turn to niche markets for specific expertise. For example, identity theft specialists know where to find artists who can replicate the holograms on ID and credit cards. — **So, do you use real specialists?**

Collaborate across borders (even with competitors)

Don't look at competitors simply as rivals. Consider the mutual benefits of partnerships. The Hong Kong – based triads and the Japanese Yakuza have joined forces to market synthetic drugs, while Colombia's cartels cooperate with Russian and Eastern European mafias to expand the reach of their products. Working cross-border also creates legal obstacles for law enforcement officials, who often aren't as adept at cross-border collaboration as the criminals they're tracking. — **Who can you work with to increase synergy?**

The perfect prefix

It's time for new terminology for your innovation challenges. Take a cue from other domains.

The perfect prefix generator allows you to systematically explore adjectives, transferring proven concepts from other sectors into your industry.

Try this:
Place the prefixes before your current innovation challenge to come up with new solutions, products or services.

Combinations

Mixed	*mixed drinks / mixed herbs / mixed-gauge railway*
Dual	*dual view / dual alarm clock / dual boot*
Hybrid	*hybrid car / hybrid energy / hybrid technology*
Functional	*functional food / functional resume / functional art*
Smart	*smart meter / smart board / smart key*

Experience

Personal	*personal coach / personal food / personal rapid transit*
Convenience	*convenience store / convenience meals / convenience packaging*
Retro	*retro candy / retro games / retro furniture*
Emotional	*emotional intelligence / emotional health / emotional geography*
Artificial	*artificial intelligence / artificial heart / artificial snow*
3D	*3D barcodes / 3D jigsaw puzzles / 3D printer*
Colored	*colored aluminium foil / colored iPod / colored refrigerators*
Mood	*mood lighting / mood music / mood tagging*
Visual	*visual dictionary / visual novel / visual thinking*
Guerrilla	*guerrilla gardening / guerrilla advertising / guerrilla learning*
Underground	*underground economy / underground art / underground eco homes*

Customer insights

Free	*free shipping / free online games / free internet phone calls*
Easy	*easyJet / easy songs for guitar / easy swim*
Self	*self service / self storage / self help books*
Transparent	*transparent bra / transparent aluminium / transparent packaging*
Invisible	*invisible tattoo / invisible glass / invisible bra*
Perfect	*perfect christmas gifts / perfect uninstaller / perfect draft*
Safe	*safe cosmetics / safe search / safe toys*
All-inclusive	*all-inclusive resorts / all-inclusive insurance / all-inclusive laundry service*
Zero	*zero tolerance / zero-coke / zero energy house*

Dimensions

Direct	*direct buy / direct democracy / direct response TV*
Micro	*micro loans / micro wind turbine / micro payment*
Multi	*multichannel retailers / multi-brand / multi-fuel stoves*
Mini	*mini beamer / mini omnium / mini triathlon*
Nano	*nanocomputing / nano car / nano battery*
Pocket	*pocket bike / pocket projector / pocket video camera*
Minimal	*minimal design / minimal jewellery / minimal music*
Low	*low budget / low-tech / low energy bulbs*
Flexible	*flexible display / flexible solar cells / flexible wall*
Foldable	*foldable bike / foldable bed / foldable water bottle*
Soft	*soft ice / software / soft jazz*
Light	*light graffiti / light rail / light menu*

People planet profit

Sustainable	*sustainable tourism / sustainable coffee / sustainable banking*
Local	*local food / local search / local currency*
Urban	*urban biking / urban art / urban vegetables*
Eco	*eco home / eco jeans / eco phone*
Slow	*slow food / slow travel / slow parenting*
Fair	*fair trade / fair presents / fair food*
Solar	*solar car / solar brick / solar jacket*

Visit <u>crossindustryinnovation.com</u> for even more perfect prefixes.

remix your industry

VALUE   **COSTS**   **IMPACT**   **...**

Remix and disrupt your industry

Many disruptive innovations come from totally different sectors.

There is hope. Instead of waiting for someone to disrupt your industry — let's see what you can do yourself.

"No candle maker has become a bulb manufacturer, no carriage maker has become a car manufacturer and the post office did not invent email."

— *Prof. Marc Giget*

We discovered 9 ways to disrupt your industry:

1. Make shortcuts
2. Challenge existing rules & regulations
3. Reduce complexity dramatically
4. Combine various types of innovation
5. Remove one crucial element
6. Cut prices by 90% or more
7. Do the opposite
8. Do impossible things
9. Blend and navigate business models

———

It's time to disrupt your industry or maybe even better… disrupt another industry.

Make shortcuts

In its time, Dell revolutionised the way personal computers were sold by going directly to the end-user and even having people pay upfront; a clear case of cutting out the middleman.

**Modern day examples
of shortcuts are online
insurances, holiday
bookings, price comparison
websites, farm-to-table,
peer-to-peer lending and
crowd funding.**

Make your own elephant path

An elephant path is an unofficial route
— a path made by people finding their
own way and coming up with their own
shortcuts.

The elephant path is an anarchic way of
moving through a city, an organisation or
software.

Concepts related to making shortcuts:
Direct-selling, disintermediation,
not-intended use, digitisation, life hacks.

Which shortcuts can you find in your
value chain or processes?

小草休寙 请勿扛揽

DO NOT DISTURB

TINY GRASS
IS DREAMING

Challenge the rules

Many industries keep thinking in silos and stay rigidly within the boundaries of present-day rules and regulations.

The ride-share application **Uber** breaks existing rules in the taxi industry with a new business model. **Airbnb** has grown into a major online accommodation booking website in a very short time. Both companies challenge authorities to change existing rules.

"Learn the rules like a pro, so you can break them like an artist." — Pablo Picasso

Question the expiry dates of rules and laws

Search pro-actively for agreements, rules and laws within your industry and try to challenge these in a *What if?*-session. For example: *"What if this rule was no longer valid?"*

"Why is Tesla legally forced to use a dealer network, while they would rather sell to customers directly?"

"Why are The Yellow Pages still distributed via an opt-out model (everybody receives one unless)? Why can't this be an opt-in product?"

The Dutch government innovation team — **InAxis** — created a *Museum of Redundant Policy* to battle rules and regulations that are repetitive, conflicting or no longer relevant.

Challenge the rules in your industry.

Dramatically reduce complexity

Simplify by:

Less buttons / one button
Senseo coffee machine, touch screen, etc.

Do it yourself
DIY pregnancy test, self-service check-in, etc.

Modular blocks
LEGO, modular block phone, etc.

Plug and play
No manual, self-installation, etc.

Standardisation
Shipping containers, universal chargers, etc.

Even simpler:

Reduction of the numbers of parts, less choice, better usability, no frills, not doing things

More inspiration on less?

Also check out the beautiful book *Less is beautiful* by **Cyriel Kortleven**.

		how you...	examples
configuration	**PROFIT MODEL**	make money	auction, subscription, freemium, etc.
	NETWORK	connect with others to create value	franchising, alliances, open innovation, etc.
	STRUCTURE	align your talents and assets	incentive systems, outsourcing, asset standardisation, etc.
	PROCESS	use signature or superior methods to do your work	localisation, crowdsourcing, lean production, etc.
offering	**PRODUCT PERFORMANCE**	employ distinguishing features and functionality	ease of use, safety, customisation, etc.
	PRODUCT SYSTEM	create complementary products and services	product bundling, extensions, closed eco-system, etc.
experience	**SERVICE**	support and enhance the value of your offerings	try before you buy, self-service, guarantee, etc.
	CHANNEL	deliver your offerings to customers and users	cross-selling, flagship store, pop-up presence, etc.
	BRAND	represent your offerings and business	co-branding, transparency, private label, etc.
	CUSTOMER ENGAGEMENT	foster distinctive interactions	curation, community and belonging, status, etc.

Combine various types of innovation

Most successful companies combine different types of innovation.

Doblin was created — by **Deloitte** — as a model to demonstrate that there are different types of innovation to choose from. In addition — within the scope of each type there are different components to play with, allowing to really remix your industry.

3 steps to learn from innovation types

Check out which types of innovation your organisation scores highest and lowest on.

Look for example companies that are really good in areas in which your organisation still has room for improvement.

See what you can learn from these top companies *(be specific, focus on the process details)*.

Remove one (important) element

Some nice examples

Cirque du Soleil *(no animals)*

Dyson vacuum cleaner *(no bag)*

Waterless toilet *(no water)*

iPod Shuffle *(no display)*

Self-driving cars *(no steering wheel)*

...

PRIX
DU CAFÉ
EN TERRASSE

UN CAFÉ	7€
UN CAFÉ, S'IL VOUS PLAÎT	4,25€
BONJOUR, UN CAFÉ, S'IL VOUS PLAÎT	1,40€

Cut prices by 90% or more

Who could have imagined 15 years ago that we would be able to call internationally for free, read free newspapers or listen to any song we choose without paying?

Skype, Spotify and Metro newspaper are just a few examples of the universe of free products and services.

3 strategies to switch to *free*

Freemium

Freemium is a pricing strategy for which a product or service *(typically digital, e.g. software, media, games or web services)* is provided free of charge — while money *(premium)* is charged for proprietary features, functionality or virtual goods. Some examples: LinkedIn, Skype, Spotify, Dropbox, etc.

————

Are you able to make a freemium version?

Add-on

The core product is priced competitively — yet the various extras drive the price up. Some examples: Low cost carriers, SAP, cheap cruises, etc.

————

Can you make a division between a basic version and add-ons?

Hidden revenue

A situation in which the user is no longer responsible for the income of the business. Instead, the main source of revenue comes from a third party. This third party cross finances whatever free or low-priced offering attracts users.

A very common example of this model is financing through advertisement, where attracted customers are of value to the advertisers who fund the offering. This concept facilitates the idea of *Separation between revenue and customer*. Some examples: JCDecaux, Metro newspaper, Google, Facebook, etc.

————

Can you find third parties who are willing to invest in your business?

welcome to

AUSTIN

LET US SHOW YOU AROUND

loku.com/atx

Do the opposite

If everybody zigs, you zag

In a world where many businesses and organisations look and act the same, a way to stand out is to do the opposite.

Learn from the street
Streetwize is a Belgian organisation which takes managers and leaders out to learn from street kids. Managers learn real survival skills in challenging environments. **Arnoud Raskin** — the founder — invests the profits in their *mobile school* project.

Ugly models
A modelling agency in London with a clear positioning opposite of its competitors:

"We like our women fat and our men geeky, we like the extremely tall and the shockingly small."

Reverse graffiti
Reverse graffiti — also known as clean tagging, dust tagging, grime writing, green graffiti or clean advertising — is a method of creating temporary or semi-permanent images on walls, floors or other surfaces by selectively removing dirt from a surface. In addition to the surprise element — another advantage is that you can actually advertise things in places where advertising is not allowed.

COCD–BOX

idea classification tool

IMPOSSIBLE TO IMPLEMENT

YELLOW IDEAS
ideas for the future
dreams, challenges
stimulation for the brain
tomorrow's red ideas

HOW?

EASY TO IMPLEMENT

BLUE IDEAS
easy to implement
low risk
high acceptability
done before

NOW!

RED IDEAS
innovative ideas
breakthrough
exciting ideas
can be implemented

WOW!

NORMAL IDEAS   **ORIGINAL IDEAS**

Do impossible things

It's impossible. You are crazy. You are dreaming...

Pioneers and explorers have been ignoring these idea killers and kept believing in their dreams, which finally led to them success.

Mark Raison — who came up with the concept of *Yellow Ideas* created the COCD box, an easy tool to help with the classification of ideas. Yellow ideas appeal to dreams and are a stimulation for the brain. Some examples of *impossible* ideas that became reality:

The ice hotel

Each year — between December and April — the world's first ice hotel in the village of **Jukkasjärvi** *(Sweden)* opens its doors.

Wikipedia

Making a free online encyclopedia that is even more accurate than any physical one using only volunteers.

Free fall

Felix Baumgartner's free fall — powered by Red Bull Stratos — set the world record for skydiving, as he jumped from a helium balloon at a height of 39 kilometres *(24 miles)*, reaching an estimated speed of 1,350 KMH. In the process, Felix also became the first person to break the sound barrier *(without use of a vehicle)*.

"Nothing is impossible, the word itself says: I'm possible."
— *Audrey Hepburn*

THE WATER IS CALLING

No experience necessary. Find the perfect boat with or without a capt

Boats In | Enter a location | 🔍 Find Boats Now

"The Airbnb for ... boats?!
Boatbound: a pier-to-pier network."

Blend business models

What's a business model like that doing in an industry like this?

The 'x' for 'y'

The *Airbnb for x* phenomenon rests on the fact that getting used to the concept of a model in one industry allows for easier adoption of the model in other industries.

When users adopt one collaborative consumption service like **Airbnb** *(new way to travel and offset housing costs)* other collaborative consumption services are more likely to be tried out, for instance **BlaBlaCar** *(new form of carpooling and offset travel costs).*

Take the following examples:

- The Airbnb for boats, cars, food, etc.
- The Netflix for beauty services, home decoration, storage, etc.
- The IKEA for road construction, schools, vacations, etc.
- The Uber for pizza delivery, home cleaning, errands, etc.
- The Tesco for jewellery, coaching, software development, etc.
- The … for …

What can a business model like yours do in an industry like mine?

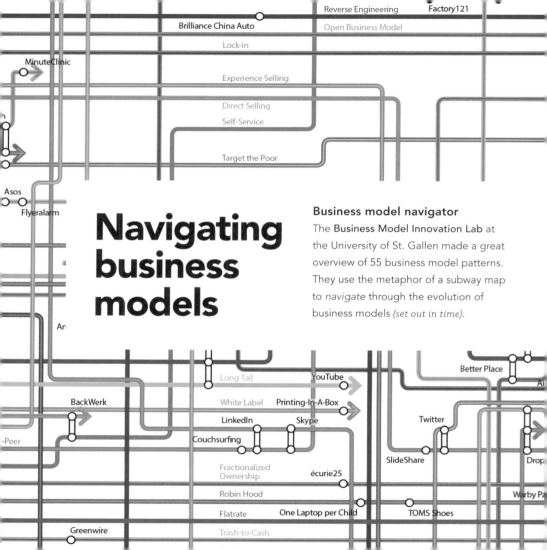

Reverse Engineering · Factory121
Brilliance China Auto · Open Business Model
Lock-in
MinuteClinic
Experience Selling
Direct Selling
Self-Service
Target the Poor
Asos
Flyeralarm

Navigating business models

Business model navigator
The Business Model Innovation Lab at the University of St. Gallen made a great overview of 55 business model patterns. They use the metaphor of a subway map to *navigate* through the evolution of business models *(set out in time)*.

An

Better Place
Long Tail · YouTube
BackWerk
White Label · Printing-In-A-Box
LinkedIn · Skype
Couchsurfing
Twitter
-Peer
SlideShare · Drop
Fractionalized Ownership · écurie25
Robin Hood
Warby Pa
Flatrate · One Laptop per Child · TOMS Shoes
Greenwire
Trash-to-Cash

The 55 business model patterns:

1. Add-on
2. Affiliation
3. Aikido
4. Auction
5. Barter
6. Cash machine
7. Cross-selling
8. Crowdfunding
9. Crowdsourcing
10. Customer loyalty
11. Digitisation
12. Direct selling
13. E-commerce
14. Experience selling
15. Flat rate
16. Fractional ownership
17. Franchising
18. Freemium
19. From-push-to-pull
20. Guaranteed availability
21. Hidden revenue
22. Ingredient branding
23. Integrator
24. Layer player
25. Leverage customer data
26. License
27. Lock-in
28. Long tail
29. Make more of it

30. Mass customisation
31. No frills
32. Open business model
33. Open source
34. Orchestrator
35. Pay per use
36. Pay what you want
37. Peer-to-peer
38. Performance-based contracting
39. Razor and blade
40. Rent instead of buy
41. Revenue sharing
42. Reverse engineering
43. Reverse innovation
44. Robin Hood
45. Self-service
46. Shop-in-shop
47. Solution provider
48. Subscription
49. Supermarket
50. Target the poor
51. Trash-to-cash
52. Two-sided market
53. Ultimate luxury
54. User designed
55. White label

Combine or transfer these models to create new solutions for your industry.

GUESS

W A T C H E S

September 11, 2014

Mr. Tim Cook
Apple, Inc.
1 Infinite Loop
Cupertino, CA 95014
USA

LETTER TO CEO OF APPLE, FROM CEO OF GUESS WATCHES

Dear Mr. Cook:

I wanted to write to you and welcome you to the Watch Industry and also offer my personal thanks to you.

As one of the largest fashion watch brands in the world, we have been around for more than 30 years. In the early 80's, there was really only SWATCH (the brand) and GUESS Watches. At that time, we had many critics who thought we were crazy. No one thought that anyone would want this new type of "novelty" timepiece. They believed that the only "real" alternatives were Swiss mechanicals or traditional quartz timepieces. Fortunately for us, consumers thought differently!

We are part of an old and proud industry. Every year we've experienced change in some way. Over these years, we have seen the introduction of quartz movements, the rise and fall of calculator watches, digitals, analogue-digitals and many many brands, both big and small. It seems that the test of time has shown that the wrist is an obvious place for both function and fashion.

Fast-forward to today and the world has changed. The proliferation of smartphones and the demand of consumers for round-the-clock connectivity have changed the way people access time. This has caused an understandable fear and challenge in our industry (even if no one likes to admit it).

We personally welcome this new challenge to remain relevant to our young, sexy and adventurous consumers who see as much importance in the device they carry and the messaging app they use, as the clothing and accessory brands they buy.

Over the past year, there has been dramatic speculation on the future of "wearables" and Apple's entre into this segment. This week, you delivered! Just as we had in the early 00's, there are naysayers and believers. I, for one, am a fan! Your innovation and attention to detail is spectacular.

In today's connected world, consumers deserve the next level of combining fashion and function. We've always been much more than a watch. Now, we too are going to take that concept even further. As we look forward to the launch of our own connected timepiece for GUESS..."Powered by MARTIAN", we're happy to have another true brand innovator in our industry that confirms the wrist as the dominant place for self-expression.

Congratulations.

Cindy Livingston
President & CEO
GUESS WATCHES

Welcome to our industry

Eventually, other companies are going to enter your industry or market, many with the objective to disrupt the current setting. Instead of being hostile, you can take a more elegant approach to this. Take the *Letter from the CEO* example.

A few days after the launch of the Apple Watch, the CEO of Guess Watches — Cindy Livingston — sent **Tim Cook** *(Apple CEO)* a letter welcoming Apple to the watch industry *(and also using*

the opportunity to pitch their own smart watch product). In any case, it is a stylish nod to the same thing that happened when Apple welcomed IBM to the PC industry over 30 years ago.

The left displays the letter written by Guess Watches to Apple in 2014 and here you see the original letter from Apple to IBM in 1981.

Who can you elegantly welcome *(and challenge)* in your industry?

type	YOUR activity to innovate	appliance
All-in-one	Paying	Channel
All-inclusive	Gaming	App
Ambient	Travelling	Box
Artificial		Brand
Augmented		Business
B2B	Cooking	Campaign
Bio-		Card
Convenience	...	Center
Cross		Cloud
Crowdsourced		Club
Customised	Farming	Community
Datadriven		Content
Direct	Advertising	Deal
DIY		Engine
Easy	Broadcasting	Experience
Eco		Festival
Emotional	Learning	Formula
Flexible		Guarantee
	Playing	

TOOL

Cross-industry jackpot

There are two ways to use *the cross-industry jackpot*

The book version

Step 1 Use one of the tables on the next pages and fill in — the activity that you wish
to innovate on — in the middle column.

Step 2 Think of a random number between 1..26
and select a random letter from the alphabet.

Step 3 Find the corresponding type *(number)* and appliance *(letter)*.

Step 4 Do this at least 7 times *(switch tables in between).*

Step 5 See which new combinations give a spark and apply that insight! **Jackpot!**

The online version

Go to <u>crossindustryinnovation.com</u> to have our smart algorithm do this for you!

Cross-industry jackpot

	type	fill in	appliance	
1	3D	paying	activation	A
2	all in one		app	B
3	ambient		appliance	C
4	artificial	gaming	application	D
5	augmented		aura	E
6	B2B	travelling	box	F
7	bio		brand	G
8	convenience	cooking	business	H
9	cross		campaign	I
10	crowsourced	farming	card	J
11	customised		centre	K
12	data-driven	advertising	cloud	L
13	direct		club	M
14	DIY	...	community	N
15	easy		concept	O
16	eco	broadcasting	content	P
17	flexible		deal	Q
18	free	learning	design	R
19	happy		engine	S
20	hybrid	playing	event	T
21	invisible		experience	U
22	local	accounting	extension	V
23	mini		fact sheet	W
24	mobile	driving	festival	X
25	modular		formula	Y
26	multifunctional	manufacturing	guarantee	Z

	Step 1	Use one of the tables and fill in — the activity that you wish to innovate on — in the middle column.
	Step 2	Think of a random number between 1..26 and select a random letter from the alphabet.
	Step 3	Find the corresponding type *(number)* and appliance *(letter)*.
	Step 4	Do this at least 7 times *(switch tables in between)*.
	Step 5	See which new combinations give a spark and apply that insight! **Jackpot!**

	type		**fill in**		**appliance**	
1	on-demand	•	phoning	•	jacket	A
2	open	•		•	lease	B
3	outdoor	•	investing	•	management	C
4	P2P	•		•	market	D
5	pay-as-you-go	•	publishing	•	mode	E
6	perfect	•		•	offering	F
7	pop-up	•	studying	•	package	G
8	portable	•		•	payment	H
9	precision	•	dining	•	plan	I
10	real time	•		•	platform	J
11	retro	•	sporting	•	product	K
12	reverse	•		•	programme	L
13	self	•	...	•	proposition	M
14	slow	•		•	resort	N
15	smart	•		•	robot	O
16	social	•	shopping	•	sales	P
17	solar	•	job searching	•	service	Q
18	sustainable	•		•	shop	R
19	temporary	•	money saving	•	software	S
20	transparent	•		•	solution	T
21	urban	•	music listening	•	subscription	U
22	user generated	•		•	swap	V
23	vertical	•	house building	•	system	W
24	viral	•		•	tool	X
25	virtual	•	retiring	•	toy	Y
26	wireless	•		•	wall	Z

CHAPTER

go
out(ro)

cross-industry innovation

department
discipline
expertise
process
branch
domain
section
division
market
region
sector
arena
area
field
unit
...

Go out(ro)

You have now come to the end of the book. This is not the end of your journey: for you, it is actually the start. In the outro we would like to give you a few last insights, tools and directions to help you along the way.

The stories, strategies and tools in this book are all geared towards helping you to increase your *match sensitivity* to make better connections. We hope *Not Invented Here* is no longer a blockade, but a building block for your own cross-industry innovation efforts.

And as we are also clearly inspired by other peoples ideas, insights and concepts, this is the place where would like to credit and thank them.

"If I have seen further than others, it is by standing upon the shoulders of giants."— *Isaac Newton*

Enjoy the journey!

____

Ramon & Marc

10 key insights

Cross-industry innovation
Cross-industry innovation is a clever way to jump-start your innovation efforts by drawing analogies and transferring approaches between contexts, beyond the borders of your own industry, sector, area or domain.

Go from best to next practices
Next practices are about new markets, new concepts, new ways of working, new products and services, smart extensions, imagination, courage and entrepreneurship.

Concept – combine – create
In order to get something useful out of another sector or area, one should master three things: the ability to conceptualise, the ability to combine and eventually make it fit.

The art of questioning
Cross-industry innovation starts with asking more & better questions. The key is to ask more beautiful questions.

Someone else has solved your problem
Select your curators, use your knowledge network and find your inspiration sources.

Draw analogies

Across various industries, many organisations struggle with the same issues; actually common challenges that are not always recognised as such. Break through the jargon.

What Would x Do?

Learn from inspiring industries and smart sectors that are innovating faster or better. Investigate how other companies tackle their business challenges and what you can learn from them.

Embrace the unexpected

For cross-industry innovation you also need to embrace the power of the unexpected to create something new. Look at: arts, nature, festivals, fun, history and even the mafia.

"Adopt what you can, adapt the rest"

Remix your industry

Many disruptive and game-changing innovations come from a completely different sector. So, disrupt another industry or disrupt your own industry using insights and business models from other sectors.

Not invented here

It's our plea to embrace other people's and other sectors' ideas and build upon them. So *Not Invented Here* actually becomes *Already Invented There.*

Now use these insights as building blocks for your challenges!

Cross-industry cheat sheet

1. Concept
2. Combine
3. Create

1	YOUR INNOVATION CHALLENGE
2	THE ART OF QUESTIONING
3	SOMEONE ELSE HAS SOLVED YOUR PROBLEM
4	INSPIRING INDUSTRIES & SMART SECTORS
5	WWXD? WHAT WOULD X DO?
6	YOUR BUSINESS CHALLENGES
7	THE POWER OF THE UNEXPECTED
8	REMIX YOUR INDUSTRY
9	GO OUT!

>
describe your innovation subject
do you focus on the right things?

>

>
generate 3 challenging questions
vary with abstraction levels

>

>
make a list of potential (re)sources
who else has dealt with something *similar* before?

>

>
find 5 sectors which are ahead in development
play with their components

>

>
look for 7 companies on how they would tackle this
find the X for Y *(on process level)*

>

>
use knowledge brokers
apply the 21 innovation principles tool

>

>
find inspiration from a totally strange sector
go beyond *not invented here*

>

>
use the 9 ways to disrupt your industry
or disrupt another industry!

>

>
make your ideas happen
ask someone to test your assumptions in a lean way

>

" HANG OUT WITH MORE
PEOPLE WHO DON'T DO
WHAT you DO. "

AUSTIN KLEON

Steal like an artist

We have also been truly inspired by the book *Steal Like An Artist.*

Austin Kleon wrote this fantastic book on the creative process. In this guide, he identifies 10 rules for unlocking your personal creativity:

1. **Steal like an artist** – *artists collect inspiration selectively*
2. **Fake it till you make it** – *stop searching, start creating*
3. **Write the book you want to read** – *you are your best audience*
4. **Use your hands** – *build things, make prototypes*
5. **Side projects and hobbies are important** – *do what you love and connect the dots later*
6. **Geography is irrelevant** – *the internet connects us all*
7. **Be nice** – *the world is a small town*
8. **Be boring** – *the only way to get stuff done*
9. **Creativity is subtraction** – *focus*

Austin Kleon does not mean *steal* as in plagiarise, skim or rip off — but rather analyse, study, credit, remix, adapt and transform. Creative work builds on what came before, and thus nothing is completely original.

Cross-industry innovation is about applying these creative principles to business and organisations. Everybody has the ability to be creative; to make new and better connections.

Thanks Austin!

Cross-industry manifesto

How to become a
cross-industry innovator?

1 CREATE a cross-industry ▼ *boosting board* for *your company*

PLAY with **WORDS PLAY** with **COMPONENTS**

②

LOOK ▶ 3 SIDEWAYS

- ask more -

beautiful questions

4 LISTEN TO NEW PEOPLE IN YOUR ORGANISATION

ALWAYS CARRY AN IDEA NOTEBOOK OR APP - - - - - - 5

6 VISIT COMPANIES From other sectors (also on your vacation)

7 ???

— **10** —
ORGANISE + **9 COMBINE** *unusual* things

CONCEPT – COMBINE – CREATE in your organisation

- do -
impossible things *** 12

read the **8 NATIONAL GEOGRAPHIC**

11 VISIT CONTEMPORARY art museums

DISCOVER THE SECRETS OF INNOVATIVE COMPANIES 13

14 COPY – ADAPT – PASTE

QUESTION 15 THINGS • (why? what if? how?)

FIND *your* INSPIRATION **curators 16**

17 Question the **ASSUMPTIONS** of your industry ?

18 - imagine - **2050**

19 FOLLOW *blogs and read magazines*

out of your **COMFORT ZONE**

20 ORGANISE 21 *a job ◀ switch ▶ day*

travel more

Ask Nature

About | Features | Participate

How does natu

EXPLORE   ...land gently

Cross-industry super sites

These 9 websites are a great starting place for cross-industry inspiration.

Visit crossindustryinnovation.com for an up-to-date and fully searchable list of 101 cross-industry super websites!

1. **springwise.com** – Springwise scans the globe for smart new business ideas, delivering immediate inspiration to entrepreneurial minds.

2. **trendwatching.com** – Global consumer trends, insights and related innovations.

3. **trendhunter.com** – The world's largest, most popular collection of cutting edge ideas, fuelled by 156,000 insatiably curious people.

4. **moreinspiration.com/search** – A really inspiring collection of 4600+ innovations searchable by keywords, industries, properties and functions.

5. **stumbleupon.com** – StumbleUpon is the easiest way to find cool new websites, videos, photos and images from across the Web.

6. **sciencechannel.com** – ScienceChannel explores outer space, engineering, cutting-edge tech, etc.

7. **ted.com** – TED is a platform for ideas worth spreading. Started in 1984 as a conference where technology, entertainment and design converged, TED today shares ideas from a broad spectrum — from science to business to global issues — in more than 100 languages.

8. **psfk.com** – Inspiring ideas to live, work and play better.

9. **asknature.org** – AskNature is a digital library of nature's solutions, organised by function, that can serve as an educational and cross-pollinating tool.

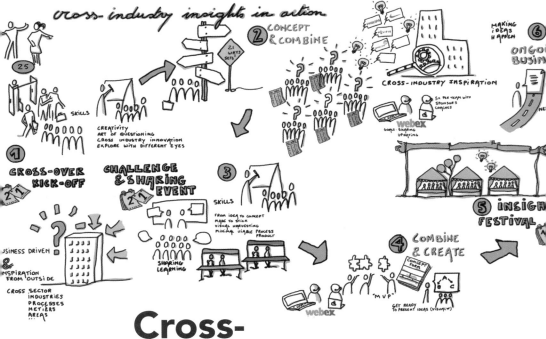

Cross-industry innovation tools & services

This is an example of a visual outline of a cross-industry project we did with one of our clients. Over the course of 6 months, we researched cross-industry insights in multiple sectors to answer strategic questions.

We believe in the free flow of ideas — which is why we share our insights on our websites, during our projects, lectures, blogs, reports, videos and in this book.

——————————

Visit the book's website, where you will find tools you can immediately use by yourself, such as a gallery of cases and examples in many industries; 101+ useful sites for starting your (re)search; downloadable high-res tool formats and multiple slideshows on cross-industry innovation. Discover it all at:

www.crossindustryinnovation.com

Join the cross-industry community
Share your cross-industry insights @ crossindustryinnovation.com and use the Twitter hashtags #xind and #innovation combined.

Where we can help to jump-start your cross-industry innovation efforts
Ramon Vullings and Marc Heleven provide the following professional cross-industry services:

- Keynotes *(with custom examples)*
- Workshops and training
- Consulting
- 21 ways sets
- Innovative web search
- ideaDJ business event boosting
- Custom image and video sets *(for brainstorming & future centres)*
- Learning programs & expeditions
- Leadership journeys

It's not where you
take things from.

It's where you
take them to.

— *Jean-Luc Godard*

Thanks

This book is infused by inspiration from many sources and we would like to thank everyone, and especially:

Our fellow authors and inspirators: Kirby Ferguson *(Everything is a Remix)*, Austin Kleon *(Steal Like An Artist)*, Frans Johansson *(The Medici Effect)*, Christoph Dürmüller & David Levin *(Zuhlke Engineering)*, David Kord Murray *(Borrowing Brilliance)*, Jeff Jarvis *(WWGD?)*, Warren Berger *(A More Beautiful Question)*, Tom Kelley *(IDEO)*, Janine Beynus *(Biomimicry)*, Lawrence Lessig *(Remix)*, Ellen Enkel *(Zeppelin University)* and Oliver Gassmann *(University of St. Gallen)*.

Our 21 Lobsterstreet colleagues: Karen van Heuckelom, Cyriel Kortleven, Martine Vanremoortele, Willem Stortelder, Johan D'Haeseleer and Joost Kadijk.

And of course…
Linda Corstjens, Kobe Heleven, Hans Kokhuis, Mark Vandael, Gijs van Wulfen, Dennis Luijer, Martin de Ruiter, Ruud Bakker, Bavo Dockx, Marjolein Huibers, Martijn van Kooij, Ruud Geers, Cosimo Turroturro, Dick van Schooneveld, Simon Schneider, Sander Mulder, Nicole van Autrève, Peter Fisk, Rudy Pont, Simon Dewulf, Marcel Grauls, Yannis De Cleene, Natacha Dagneaud, Karl Raats, Katrin Schwabe, Nicole van den Bosch, Daphne Depasse, Stien Michiels, David Hespe, Flanders District of Creativity, the Center for Creativity Development *(COCD)*, Fontys University of Applied Sciences and the Antwerp Management School.

TIP: Google these names… they'll lead you to other beautiful areas and insights.

Image credits

References

p.8 Remix — Lawrence Lessig

p.13 zuehlke.com/uploads/tx_zepublications/124_cd_european_ceo_cross_innovation.pdf

p.13-15 onlinelibrary.wiley.com/doi/10.1111/j.1467-9310.2010.00591.x/abstract

p.21 ramonvullings.com/services/key-note-speaker/applied-creativity

p.29 idea-sandbox.com/resources/idea_killer_bingo.pdf

p.39,44 slideshare.net/rsm/the-art-of-powerful-questions-16351697

p.42 The Right Question Institute

p.52 creativitytoday.net

p.59 7ideas.net/cross-industry

p.71 financesonline.com/10-disappearing-jobs-that-wont-exist-in-10-years-professions-that-wont-guarantee-career-opportunities/

p.72 linkedin.com/pulse/article/20140425065253-206580-50-dead-products-and-5-tips-to-stay-off-this-list

p.75 mashable.com/2014/04/28/jobs-of-the-future/

p.75 compassioninpolitics.wordpress.com/2011/08/14/30-billion-dollar-industries-of-the-future/

p.85 mentalfloss.com/article/31510/9-things-invented-military-use-you-now-encounter-everyday-life

p.85 mandatory.com/2012/10/23/10-everyday-items-we-can-thank-the-military-for-inventing/10

p.87 wired.com/2014/05/formula-1-steering-wheels

p.89 fastcocreate.com/3027892/delta-wants-to-put-you-on-a-flight-with-an-inspirational-business-leader

p.93 trendhunter.com/trends/future-of-fashion1

p.95 thecasecentre.org/educators/products/view?id=101283

p.96 spinoff.nasa.gov/

p.107 15inno.com/wp-content/uploads/2013/02/Open-Innovation-at-LEGO1.pdf

p.107 entrepreneur.com/article/227746

p.109 blog.guykawasaki.com/2012/04/10-things-you-can-learn-from-the-apple-store.html

p.115 supercompressor.com/home/things-you-didn-t-know-about-ikea-12-interesting-facts-about-ikea

p.121 boardofinnovation.com/free-downloads

p.132 gartner.com/technology/supply-chain/top25.jsp

p.139 thefuntheory.com

p.156 en.wikipedia.org/wiki/Mercedes-Benz_Bionic

p.159 stoweboyd.com/post/48533957128/janine-benyus-9-basic-principles-of-biomimicry

p.168 hbr.org/2011/11/what-business-can-learn-from-organized-crime/ar/1

p.185 doblin.com/tentypes

p.193 yellowideas.com/index.php?option=com_content&view=article&id=85&Itemid=84

p.197 im.ethz.ch/education/HS13/MIS13/Business_Model_Navigator.pdf

p.213 austinkleon.com/steal/

"No more excuses for not being a leader in innovation! In Not Invented Here Ramon and Marc inspire and challenge you to innovate your company. They show you the way and the tools you need, such as the 21 practical innovation principles. A real fun and valuable book."

Annette Nijs — *Executive Director Global Initiative China Europe International Business School (CEIBS) and former Dutch Cabinet Minister for Education, Science and Culture*

"Can't imagine how boring my life would have been if every industry had limited themselves to their own innovative ideas. Ramon and Marc really nicely visualize and explain the leaps we've taken over the past decade(s), which makes cross-industry innovation an exciting teaser of what might be ahead of us..."

Peter Lathouwers — *Director Business Intelligence, Nike Europe*

"If you have a business challenge and you do not know what to do, Ramon and Marc have an answer with Not Invented Here. This book encourages you to consider the possibility that someone else might already have solved your problem."

Tanyer Sonmezer — *Group CEO of Management Centre Turkey*

"The more you are an expert in your own business, the more you need a cross-industry view in order to go beyond best practices and finding next practices. Asking the right questions and having the will to accept 'nearlings' will remain key in our learning approach. I felt that reading this book was much like working with Ramon & Marc: inspiring, joyful and always ready to start learning all over again in search for new insights."

Nicole Van Autrève — *Head of Learning & Development, GDF SUEZ Energy Europe*

"Not Invented Here will open your eyes and mind for cross-industry innovation! Get this book and you'll find a powerful toolbox for innovating your business model. Not Invented Here gets to the point and is a guide to getting started immediately. Stop talking; start innovating! Congratulations to Ramon & Marc: great job!"

Andreas Hinkelmann — *CEO of Grupo ecoEnergias del Guadiana*